SATURDAY NIGHT LIVE:

EQUAL OPPORTUNITY OFFENDER

The Uncensored Censor

SATURDAY NIGHT LIVE:
EQUAL OPPORTUNITY OFFENDER

The Uncensored Censor

by

William G. Clotworthy

1stBooks - rev. 3/16/01

How well Horatius kept the bridge.

—Lays of Ancient Rome, **Horatius**, Stanza 27

We're not Horatius, but Lord knows, we tried.

Dedication

For: Ralph, Rick, Maurie and Dick
Whose belief in the highest moral and ethical standards on
television,
in society and in their personal lives, remains an inspiration.

In Memory of
Travie

A censor is a man who knows more than
he thinks you ought to.
—**Laurence J. Peter**, 1977

I'm the guy a lot of people thought didn't exist. I was the one who decided how much painted-on pubic hair could be shown on a nude statue on national television. It was my responsibility to define how large a bull's balls could be and still get on the air. And I saved the world from watching comedian Sam Kinison imitate a homosexual necrophiliac.

I'm the man they called "Doctor No," the network censor on *Saturday Night Live*, at that time the most provocative and controversial program on television. Many times I'd meet someone at a cocktail party who'd react when I told them my vocation. "You mean there is one on that show?!!" All I could reply was, "You should see what didn't get on the air!"

That's what a lot of this book is about — what a censor is supposed to do — what he actually accomplishes — and how he makes decisions, all in the context of my long career in the broadcasting business, from NBC Page in 1948 to Director of Broadcast Standards for NBC in 1979 until 1991 when I left to become a consultant, the modern network euphemism for "retiree."

The word "censor" is in itself a euphemism as we referred to ourselves as "editors." Censorship, by definition, is the "restriction of any expression believed to threaten the political, social or moral order." Well, we weren't involved with military secrets, merely television entertainment. *Married, with Children, Saturday Night Live*, not even *Jerry Springer* are threats to the political order although there are some religious and conservative Special Interest Groups that consider them a threat to the moral!

Then, too, "censor" conjures up a picture of a pinch-faced prude with a green eye shade and a blue pencil operating with a rack of cast-iron values upon which each work must fit, making no effort to judge a work by its intention or possible effect. He just strips it of bumps and lumps and makes it conform to a mold.

That attitude was personified by the anal-retentive little censor played by Tim Kazurinsky on Weekend Update. His

1

name, Worthington Clotman, was a deliberate variation of mine although I failed to see any resemblance to a character who was so shifty and constricted that he reminded one of the old canard that censors are "paid to have dirty minds." If that's the case, then *Saturday Night Live* made my job very easy.

HOST DON RICKLES (AT UPDATE DESK)
And now we have an editorial by the vice president in charge of Standards and Practices here at NBC, Mr. Worthington Clotman. Mr. Clotman.

TIM (SEATED NEXT TO DON)
Thank you, Mr. Rickles. Taste on television seems to be a thing of the past. Today we are inundated with racial slurs, sexual innuendoes and a total disregard for privacy. Nothing is sacred. This is particularly true in the case of the so-called insult comedians. It is very bad taste to talk about a short person that, because of his stature, dogs are liable to compare him with a toilet facility. Insult comedians on television seem to feel they can freely refer to a person's race, creed or national origin in any derogatory manner. Tonight I've had to censor on this show comments maligning Jews, Catholics, Italian, Poles, homosexuals and Mr. Frank Sinatra who has never killed anyone. And President and Mrs. Reagan who've been described as drooling, belching old geezers with no control of their vital organs. This frontal assault on our sensibilities must stop. Comedy on television should entertain, not offend, and insult comedians should be funny instead of shocking. Especially a certain fat little bald Jew from Las Vegas who should wear a truss over his head as a muzzle, and shall remain nameless.

RICKLES

Thank you, Mr. Clotman. (GRABS TIMMY AND STRANGLES HIM)

***

With that kind of reputation, one may well ask why anyone would want to be a censor, the man everyone loves to hate. Believe me, there's no lining up to be one. In my case it was mid-life crisis. I was employed by a large advertising agency, working for a "mad genius" who was unappreciative of my many talents, or so I thought. In other words, it was time for a change and when I was approached by an old friend at NBC about a job in Broadcast Standards, I was receptive, asking why he thought I could handle that kind of specialized work. "Well, Bill, you've been around the business a long time. You have experience which is very important. Second, you've always exhibited good judgment. And, third, you've shown a remarkable ability to get along with crazy people!"

Gee, thanks a lot.

He was referring, of course, to the creative community; actors, writers and producers who, it is true, are temperamental, opinionated, difficult, intransigent, maddening, egotistical and, every so often, right. But I love them because of their idiosyncrasies, just as I am jealous of their talent and free spirit. After all, I was a professional square, a naysayer, the only guy at meetings wearing a suit and tie, a conservative. My God, I'm even a WASP! And never allowed to forget it.

This all happened when I was in my mid-50s and had spent most of my career with the advertising agency BBDO which stood for Batten, Barton, Durstine and Osborn, a distinguished company with a list of prestigious national clients. One claim to their fame was Jack Benny's (actually Mary Livingstone's) famous on-air joke that Batten, Barton, Durstine and Osborn sounded like a trunk falling down a flight of steps!

3

In the 1950s, sponsors controlled television programming and as a result I spent time working as sort of a censor for the clients, keeping an eye on programs they sponsored. I transferred to BBDO's Hollywood office in 1953 where my primary client representation was for the General Electric Company, then sponsoring a weekly Hollywood-produced dramatic anthology, *General Electric Theatre*, hosted by actor Ronald Reagan.

Unlike *Saturday Night Live, GE Theatre* didn't set out to push the envelope of taste, not by a long shot. The biggest brouhaha I can remember was over a show in which actress Simone Signoret appeared to be scantily dressed during a bedroom scene with Lee Marvin. That worried GE a little, but what really caused a flap was when Marvin's character lost his temper and broke a table radio. That, to General Electric, was a true obscenity and I was ordered to make sure the nation's television viewers were spared the horror of appliance abuse. And God forbid that a kitchen set be equipped with a gas range!

My main responsibility, however, was to write and produce host Reagan's introductions — "Good evening. Tonight the *General Electric Theatre* presents the television debut of Edward G. Robinson. Mr. Robinson appears in an original teleplay..." well, they were pretty much the same each week, as predictable as they could be with only the names changed to protect the innocent.

We normally shot those gems at the end of the day, piggybacking on the set of some show that had completed its day's work, such as *Leave it to Beaver*. I was always amused by the fact that Beaver's standin for lighting purposes was a midget. Makes sense as the midget was an adult who could work a full day whereas child actors were restricted in the number of hours they could work.

In any event, we often we had to wait for an available stage, consequently I spent many hours in Reagan's dressing room while he practiced his latest GE plant tour speech. He constantly talked politics as a concerned private citizen, introduced me to the *National Review* and right wing politics, was the first person

4

I ever saw wearing contact lenses and always had the freshest jokes, often ethnic or vulgar. I was amused by the flap in New Hampshire during a primary campaign when he was criticized for telling an ethnic story. People forget that actors love ethnic humor, not because they are racist but because they love to perform, especially to show off their mastery of accents! Ronald Reagan didn't have a mean bone in his body. He may have been a bullshitter but apparently ethnic jokes are considered in a different light when one's a presidential candidate.

I remember one year when there was a mayoral race in Los Angeles pitting Norris Poulson against Sam Yorty and I remarked to Reagan, "You're always yapping about politics, now here's the perfect spot for you, Mayor of LA. Why don't you run?" He looked at me for a moment and waved his hand dismissively, "Mayor of LA? Nah, it's president or nothin'!" When he finally did run, for governor and then president, people were inclined to dismiss him as just another actor, conveniently forgetting his terms as president of the Screen Actors Guild and his deep political interest and activism. People at the studio were likely to think of Ronald Reagan as a crashing bore rather than a viable political animal, the exceptions being Lew Wasserman and Taft Schreiber of MCA, Reagan's agents and Hollywood power brokers who sold Reagan to the California State Republican party as a candidate for governor even as he was changing political affiliation from registered Democrat!

I look back on my time spent with the Reagans with fondness and deep respect. Ron and Nancy were invariably pleasant and gracious, and it was early in our relationship that Ron taught me a lesson in domestic politics. Whenever he came to the studio from home or ranch, he'd immediately call Nancy to tell her he'd arrived. When we'd finished our work, he'd call again to say he was on his way home. And he always, but always, terminated the call by expressing his love. "I love you, Mommie," and admonished me if I neglected to do the same. "But, Ron, I'm going to be home in twenty minutes!" "It doesn't matter, Bill. Women want to know you love them, and you can't repeat it too often!" Later, on the campaign trail and even into his presidency, there were jokes about Nancy's apparently slavish attention to his speeches and their "corny" devotion to each other. As I write this, in the autumn of 2000, Nancy's book, *I Love You, Ronnie*, has just been published. The book, filled with his love letters and her poignant reflections, has been called "A Great American Love Story" and I, for one, can personally confirm that their relationship was just that. They were <u>always</u> like that.

General Electric Theatre itself was an interesting experience. The producer was a middle-aged dilettante, Bill Frye, friend and confidante to many major Hollywood stars, especially fading leading ladies. We introduced so many to television that the show was referred to as "Menopause Theatre." Joan Crawford, Madeline Carroll, Ann Harding, Joan Fontaine, Rosalind Russell, Claire Trevor, Bette Davis, Merle Oberon, Tallulah Bankhead, Claudette Colbert, Gene Tierney, Barbara Stanwyck and Irene Dunne all starred on *General Electric Theatre*.

Actually *General Electric Theatre* was a classy dramatic anthology, bringing to television works of such eminent writers as Thomas Hardy, Sherwood Anderson, Stephen Vincent Benet, Henrik Ibsen and many more. And the male stars weren't bad, either — James Dean, Alan Ladd, James Stewart, Paul Muni, Charles Laughton, Fred Astaire, Edward G. Robinson, Ray Milland, The Marx Brothers (!) and, of course, Ronald Reagan himself.

General Electric Theatre was produced by Revue Productions, owned at that time by entertainment behemoth MCA. The studio was located on the old Republic lot in North Hollywood, once the hangout for Hopalong Cassidy, Gene Autry, Roy Rogers, their buddies and their hosses. With the success of *General Electric Theatre* and other shows, MCA was able to expand, purchasing Universal Studios, a major lot in a state of financial descendency. Almost immediately Revue had developed a thriving film and television community producing

6

Leave it to Beaver, *The Real McCoys*, and many others, all utilizing the acting, producing, directing and writing clients of MCA.

Universal City, built on the Universal Studio lot, is now one of Hollywood's most popular tourist attractions, but its genesis was humble, almost accidental. In the early 50s there were no formal studio tours; only Gray Line buses were allowed on the lot, the tourists disembarking for a walkthrough of an empty soundstage, otherwise they stayed on the bus, snapping pictures of Cary Grant's parking place or a teamster driving a "honeywagon" to the back lot.

One of the programs on the lot was *Riverboat* that starred a hambone named Darren McGavin. Occasionally McGavin would board a tour bus to schmooze with the folks and pass out publicity stills. Of Darren McGavin, of course. A young studio flunky witnessed McGavin's enthusiastic reception and came up with the bright idea of selling "short ends," scraps of exposed film or outtakes, as souvenirs — at a buck a foot. He'd jump on the bus, go into a sales spiel and sell yards of perfectly worthless film otherwise destined for the dumpster. Thus it occurred to the powers-that-be that if the public had a collective orgasm meeting Darren McGavin, and would spend good money for a short end, they'd buy almost anything, and Universal City became a reality. The first step was to level a mountain on the back lot, a job that became yet another revenue source as each truckload of dirt was sold to the State of California as fill for the roadbed of the Pasadena Freeway!

Oh, they were efficient! They once tried to sell us a program called *Convoy*, an adventure series about North Atlantic convoys during World War II and the people making that perilous journey. I questioned how they could possibly come up with enough dramatic plot lines for a show confined to ships crossing from point A to point B and back again? "Heck, we've got 120 *Wagon Trains* in the can. We'll just change the covered wagons to Liberty ships!"

7

None of this prepared me for *Saturday Night Live* as there's no training course for fledgling network censors. I followed my predecessor around for a couple of weeks before he turned the responsibility, gratefully, over to me. I confess I had never seen *Saturday Night Live* before I was hired to police it. After all, watching television at 11:30 PM on Saturday night was hardly an entertainment activity for a middle-aged husband and father. Now I had to be in the studio on Saturday night, dragging home at 3 AM on Sunday morning, a schedule that didn't help my family relationships.

Fortunately (for my sanity), *Saturday Night Live* was on the air live for only twenty shows a season because of the back-breaking (and mind-numbing) schedule, a pace impossible to continue on a regular weekly basis:

1. On Monday the guest host for the following Saturday's show would meet with the writing staff, a chance for the writers to determine his/her personality and to discuss possible sketch ideas.
2. All day Monday (and night) and Tuesday (and night) the writers would be creating. Quite often they would call on me with "Can we?" questions, though not often enough.
3. On Wednesday, never before 3 PM, there was a table reading of approximately 30 sketches. The reading was attended by the producer, director, cast, writing staff, set designers, orchestra leader, music coordinator, lighting director, technical director and other assorted production personnel. Following the read-through, I would meet with associate producer Audrey Dickman, providing her with general preliminary notes, pointing out which might be problem sketches or areas of concern. More often than not, that proved to be an exercise in frustration.
4. Following the read-through, a select group — producer, director, host, head writer and a few others (not the censor) — met to choose nine or ten sketches for final

production. That meeting went on until the wee hours. When firmed up, the chosen scripts were distributed to the set designer who began work. Now he and his staff began their all-nighters.

5. On Thursday morning I found out, for the first time, which sketches were scheduled for production. Sometimes it was good news, more often than not I discovered a "Nude Beach" (later) and began to search for the writer, who by this time was usually home asleep. Producer Lorne Michaels generally turned over initial production responsibilities to the writer(s) of the individual sketches which meant interface with Standards, although the most bitter differences ended up with meetings in Lorne's office. Producer Jean Doumanian, in her one season, took a more active role with Standards, as did Producer Dick Ebersol. In any event, Thursday was "argument and rehearsal day" as they blocked the non-set types of thing — musical acts, stand-up routines, promos and the like. Sketch rehearsals had to wait for sets to be built and shipped in from NBC's Brooklyn carpentry shop. Thursday was a long day, ending around 10 PM.

6. Friday was brutal — arguments continued, rewrites took place, and camera blocking went on from early afternoon until 10 PM.

7. Saturday was unbelievable. A stop-and-go run-through began at 1 PM and continued until 5 PM, which doesn't sound too tough, except that the writers were still (or perhaps beginning) writing the host's monologue and, of course, we still hadn't seen News Update. News Update head writer Herb Sargent and the anchorman were holed up somewhere perusing Saturday's newspapers while simultaneously watching the Seven o'clock News for the most up-to-date stories. Then they wrote some fresh jokes. All that, plus a dinner break, happened between 5 PM and 8 PM. Dinner, incidentally, was always

9

interesting. It was served buffet style, catered by the finest services in New York. It featured a variety of salads, vegetables, sliced roasts, fancy pastries, gourmet ice cream and fine wines (not allowed to cast members!) I'll say one thing about Lorne Michaels. He had gourmet taste and didn't care how he spent NBC's money. Sometimes the guest host had dinner brought to the dressing room, but often joined the rest of us. It was exciting to dine with Mayor Ed Koch, Elliot Gould, Burt Reynolds or Candice Bergen. Especially Candice Bergen.

At around 8 PM there was a dress rehearsal that might last until 10, at which time I had my last chance to comment, revise or scream about anything, because almost immediately the doors closed on a crash meeting in Lorne's office (no censor allowed) in which, more often than not, he changed everything. Well, not everything, but he invariably revised the sequence of sketches (the ones with the best reaction at dress rehearsal went up front), made cuts in some sketches and additions to others (The production assistants were running changes to the cue card staff and actors while the director was meeting with the camera crew to change all their shots.) It was a madhouse.

And the clock moved inexorably to 11:30.

Director Dave Wilson: "Fade up…"

The Censor: "Now let us pray…"

It will come as no surprise that the relationship between Broadcast Standards and any program, especially *Saturday Night Live*, is adversarial. We did our best to keep things civilized, even friendly; we had to work together, but an editor can't kid himself; he is tolerated, not loved nor appreciated. When I'd veto a sketch the reaction was invariably one of shock and disbelief. "You've got to be kidding — we can't do that?" was a line I heard to death. The other favorite excuses were "But we've started to build the set!" or "I'm going to call Brandon" (Tartikoff, President of the Network) or "Let's see how it plays in dress" and the ever popular "But they said it on Carson/ LA Law/ Fox!" (Pick one.) I always tried to keep an open mind and an open door as any decision was open to debate. Such debates often went on for hours, sometimes days, and occasionally weeks, which is how I got into discussing such absurdities as how much pubic hair can be shown on a nude statue or how much of a guy's ass could be shown in a sketch set in a proctologist's office. The answer to both was "not much."

Speaking of absurdities, it was embarrassing to arrive home late and have the little woman ask what happened at the office — "Well, the writers came up with a spoof commercial for a product called 'Peenie Pads,' sort of a male sanitary napkin to be used after a trip to the men's room when the last dribble had spotted one's pants...and we had a two-hour argument over whether we could actually show the stain or just allude to it."

A college degree and thirty years in the business for that?

Inevitably the loudest yelps of protest came from the youngest writers, the ones who'd just graduated from college, recycling the juvenile sketches they'd written for the Princeton Triangle Club or Harvard's Hasty Pudding Show — suffering from the romantic illusion that they could write whatever they damn well pleased.

"First Amendment! First Amendment!" they'd cry as soon as a sketch was rejected. "Wake up and smell the coffee, boys," I'd say, "this is network television." The fact of life in television is that you cannot say whatever you want. The medium is just too powerful. Too many people can be hurt. There are too many points of view out there, too many definitions of obscenity, too many opportunities for misinterpretation, too much potential for spreading hate. Of course we cared about creative freedom and we did everything possible to let *Saturday Night Live* have it, but there were limits and it was our job to define those limits. Writer Al Franken used to say that my only function on the show was to take out all the jokes. He was kidding. I think.

I was there to keep people from getting so angry with NBC that they'd quit watching, but I make no apologies for being the one who tried to maintain some sort of balance between the right of free speech and the right not to be assaulted by offensive garbage coming out of the television screen — there's plenty of that in motion picture theaters without having it in the home as well. The Broadcast Standards editor is merely trying to make television acceptable to the majority of a large and culturally diverse national audience and, not incidentally, keep the Congress, the Federal Communications Commission and several hundred Special Interest Groups off the back of his network.

Part of the job was political. Every radio and television station in the country is licensed by the FCC to "broadcast in the public interest," and it's the editor's job to perform a delicate balancing act between the efforts of the creative people who produce programs and the expectations and tastes of the audience, so he's carrying out a kind of preventive censorship — the thoughtful and reasonable screening of brutality, obscenity, racism, religious blasphemy and other offenses. The process, then, is quite different from "censorship," for the editor listens, thinks, and decides, relatively free to apply considerations of taste unrestricted by the pressure of artificial boundaries and categories. Yes, broadcast standards have evolved from the days when the sign on one vice-president's' desk read, "When in doubt, take it out!"

The most difficult part of the job was saying "No!" because we had great respect for the creative mind and an appreciation of the talent and effort that went into the final product. There were arguments and discussions and re-writes and tantrums and more re-writes — and there were compromises. Then there was a final decision by the Broadcast Standards Department, a decision that could not be overturned by the program executive, the producer, not even by top management. Making such decisions was often painful, thankless and definitely friendless, but it sure made the job interesting!

Primarily, there was consideration of the public, a fickle bunch indeed, for they want things that are incompatible. They want the protection of what is socially desirable and the programming of which is socially undesirable. For example on *Touched by an Angel* or *Cosby,* they appreciate the reaffirmation of positive values such as love and honesty and truth. At the same time they were fascinated by the portrayal of hate and dishonesty on *Dallas.* So folks watch not only as parents, Blacks, Hispanics, or whatever, but as ordinary people hungry for diversion, for something to make them forget their own problems, for something to fire their imaginations. In other words, the public interest includes that which interests the public. Thus the editor's job is to ensure delivery of that information, excitement and pleasure without crossing the boundary of propriety and good taste while at the same time protecting the artistic integrity of the producer, writer and actors.

So where does the editor obtain the information on which he bases his decision? Well, there's input from affiliate stations that monitor viewer concerns in over 200 communities. There are phone calls (Oh boy, there are phone calls!) and thousands of letters each year (Oh boy, there are letters!) There are press clippings and studies and meetings with Special Interest Groups and outside consultants, all providing fodder for the editor's mental mill.

Of course no one wants constant government interference or monitoring, so the broadcast industry developed a system of self-regulation in which each network polices itself, hopefully assuring adherence to sensible restrictions, thus providing the public with responsible entertainment and honest advertising. The Broadcast Standards Department defines the limits of taste, tempers creative overkill, adjudicates disagreements and makes final judgments.

There is a wide range of no-nos included in written codes that cover a wide range of topics from treatment of animals to the portrayal of hypnotism. The most important and obvious, of course, are sex, violence, stereotyping, language, drugs and the treatment of controversial subjects. As the guidelines are general, they must be interpreted within the context of each individual program, taking into consideration the dramatic or comedic thrust, audience composition and expectation, time period, management policies, affiliate sensibilities, advertiser interests and possible government concerns. The NBC guideline for sex, for example, reads "Sexual scenes must be sensitively handled and contribute to plot or characterization. Gratuitous or overly explicit sexual action is unacceptable and the depiction of physical coercion intended to satisfy prurient interests is to be avoided."

So much for Amy Fisher, Lorena Bobbitt and Monica Lewinsky.

Well, maybe I'm being a bit unfair, as Broadcast Standards had oversight only over the Entertainment Division of the network. The Sports and News Divisions were exempt from our loving care.

Anyway, keeping all of those serious matters in mind, I became the Broadcast Standards editor on *Saturday Night Live,* where I found myself making such monumental decisions as to how big a bull's scrotum could be in a spoof of a Merrill Lynch commercial — or whether the following movie promo was acceptable:

OPEN ON: PHOTO OF AN OMINOUS LOOKING DOOR
MUSIC: HORROR MOVIE MUSIC
JULIA (V.O., BREATHLESS)

Yes, yes, yes, yes, yes (PAUSE) No. Oh, no, not again! Can't you control yourself?

PARDO (V.O.)

Zenith Pictures presents...The Premature Ejaculator. Coming too soon to a theater near you!

FADE OUT

The answer was "no."

That call was easy, but the job can be daunting, for the editor feels pressure from everywhere. Ronald Reagan used to say, "Everyone has two businesses, their own and show business" • and that's true. Not only is everyone a critic, but everyone has a television agenda. The educator wants TV to be a classroom. Preachers expect a catechism. Advertisers want a marketplace. Broadcasters expect a money machine. Special Interest Groups see TV as an image-maker. Producers want it to be theater or cinema. Newspapers want it to just go away, and at the other end, the viewer searches for what he bought the set for in the first place, entertainment and diversion.

While the beleaguered editor must be aware of those desires, he must never forget that he represents the latter — the audience. He's the viewer's advocate, trained to see the raw material through the eyes and prejudices of the viewers themselves. Thus he becomes Black, Hispanic, Italian, and Polish. He becomes Protestant, Jewish, Catholic and Muslim. He becomes Gay, Straight, Rich and Poor. Parent, Child, Old and Disabled.

> • Possibly borrowed from Oscar Wilde, "I'd much rather discuss someone else's business than my own."

Unfortunately, most people think that there are no rules; that the editor works in a vacuum. Not true. The major networks all talk a good game and even Fox pretends to police their programs, so here's what NBC publishes as their policy. Put your boots on, it's getting deep:

> "It is NBC's goal to provide programming that is consistent in quality, integrity, and entertainment value. To support that goal, NBC's Program Standards guidelines reflect an appreciation of fundamental

15

elements of taste and propriety and an understanding of our viewers and their expectations.

NBC serves a vast national audience which mirrors the rich diversity of backgrounds, customs and tastes found across our country. This audience is composed ultimately of individuals, each of whom makes viewing selections and reacts to programs from his or her own unique perspective. NBC's Program Standards are designed to accommodate these diverse interests and sensitivities.

Our viewers have come to expect NBC to provide a wide selection of programs that present positive values, stimulate thought, and entertain without causing embarrassment or harm. By providing quality television entertainment which aims to meet those expectations, NBC best serves its audience, affiliated stations and advertisers. Therefore Broadcast Standards guidelines have been developed to provide a framework for writers, actors, directors and producers to continue to create innovative and entertaining programming which respects the sensibilities of our audience.

These Program Standards guidelines are general statements of principle. Their successful application to any particular program involves inherently subjective judgments. Additionally, the environment of current taste and sensitivity is constantly undergoing subtle shifts. Therefore, when Program Standards guidelines are implemented, each program is evaluated, taking onto consideration such factors as intended or established audience, research information, viewer feedback, and time of day a particular program is intended for broadcast.

While these policies and standards apply to all programs, special standards have been developed for certain programs in recognition of the needs or sensitivities of their particular audiences. For example, there are special standards guidelines for Saturday morning children's programs.

Clearly these policies have evolved from our experience as conscientious broadcasters. NBC has a long tradition of responsible self-regulation and will continue to ensure that its programming reflects standards that merit the acceptance and trust of our viewers."

Note the key words — Integrity. Responsible. Quality. Respect. Conscientious.

Translation: We'll push the envelope as far as we can in order to attain high ratings and major profits — and keep those boobs in Congress off our back!

It's interesting to note that NBC formed the first Broadcast Standards Department in 1934! Even back then Congress and the public were pressuring the industry to clean up its act, although I'm hard-pressed to imagine what sin prompted these admonitions:

"EXPLOITATION OF CRIMINAL NEWS: Appearances or dramatizations of persons featured in current criminal or morbidly sensational news stories are not acceptable.

SOUND EFFECTS: Horrifying sound effects, unessential to plot development or calculated to mislead, shock or unduly alarm the listener, shall not be used.

DEATH: The death of any character shall not be represented in any manner shocking to the sensibilities of the public. No character shall be depicted in death agonies."

Remember, this was radio, when the only "death agony" was some unseen actor going "AARRGGHH!" into the microphone. We've come a long way, baby.

Or have we? Acceptability in many areas has changed, but not necessarily for the better. Has the constant and gratuitous use of the word "fuck" in motion pictures really contributed to dramatic progress? Or is it the pitiful manifestation of modern writers' inability to provide meaningful dialogue? Or worse yet, is it a reflection of society's descent into coarseness, bad taste and lack of respect for our language? There is, after all, quite a difference between Shakespeare's "A pox on your house" and "Up your ass, motherfucker!"

NBC once stated for the record, "Since marriage and the family are recognized and approved institutions of our society, respect for the sanctity of marriage and the home must be maintained." Today's policy, however, makes no reference to marriage, only..."our viewers have come to expect NBC to provide a wide selection of programs that present positive values, stimulate thought, and entertain without causing embarrassment or harm...the current taste and sensitivity is undergoing subtle shifts..."

Some subtle shifts, or haven't you been watching the bed-jumping all over the soaps and in prime time lately? Can we even imagine what the network was thinking in the 1930s when it trumpeted "Adultery, or free love, when the theme is essential to the plot, shall not be presented as attractive or glamorous, nor should they be subjects for comedy, for thus ridicule is cast upon the essential relationships of home, family and marriage and illicit relationships are made to seem permissible and socially acceptable."

Good grief.

So anyway, the poor square of an editor is faced with multiple moral decisions—pushed and pulled by management, producers, special interests — and his own gut. T'ain't easy, McGee.

There was a story, perhaps apocryphal, that Bob Wright, president of NBC, in discussing the dissolution of the Broadcast Standards Department, said, "Why not? Anyone can take 'shit' out of a script." Of course that's true. Even Bob Wright is familiar with the word, but only a trained editor can look at a script, then juggle the interests of management, advertisers, governmental bodies, a national audience, special interests and a vocal creative community without alienating, offending or disappointing one of them. But that's the editor's art — and we'll explore some of the things that editors face — problems with language, violence, drugs, sex, stereotyping and controversial subjects within the context of constantly shifting sands of popular taste and social acceptability.

Stay tuned.

William G. Clotworthy

Obscenity is whatever gives a judge an erection.
— **Anonymous**

When RCA established the National Broadcasting Company in 1926 they did so with publication of a self-serving mandate:

> "Any use of radio transmission which causes the public to feel that the quality of programs is not the highest, that the use of radio is not the broadest and best use in the public interest, that it is used for political advantage or selfish power, will be detrimental to the public interest in radio, and therefore to the Radio Corporation of America — the purpose of the (National Broadcasting Company) will be to provide the best programs available for broadcasting in the United States."

The framers of that pledge could not visualize in their wildest dreams *The Gong Show*, local access cable television and certainly not *Saturday Night Live*. They could not have foreseen the effect of television on American life and, as a matter of fact, they may not have foreseen television. And they certainly couldn't predict Howard Stern, Don Imus, Jerry Springer, Jim and Tammy Bakker, Rush Limbaugh nor "Nude Beach," one of the more notorious sketches on *Saturday Night Live*. Here's an excerpt:

OPEN ON: SUNNY PRIVATE BEACH AREA.
DISSOLVE TO: BEACHSIDE BAR. KEVIN, PHIL, DENNIS AND EXTRAS ARE SEATED AT THE BAR MAKING SMALL TALK. THEY ALL APPEAR NUDE, BUT ARE BLOCKED FROM THE WAIST DOWN BY THE BAR, SHRUBBERY, EVEN A GUITAR. DANA AND CARL ENTER.

CARL
I feel a little self-conscious, Tom. I mean, I've never been to a nude beach before.

DANA

Don't worry about it. Really. It's the most natural thing in the world. C'mon, I'll introduce you to some of the guys. Hey, guys!

KEVIN

Hey, Tom! Hey, your penis looks great today.

DANA

Thanks, Jack. Yours, too. Hey, Ted! How's your penis?

JON

Not bad.

DANA

Hey, I'd like you guys to meet Doug.

KEVIN

Hey, Doug. Pretty small penis there.

DENNIS

Yeah, you could pick a lock with that thing.

KEVIN

Hey, that's okay. There's plenty of guys around here with small penises. Bill's got one. Hey, Bill, come over here and show him your penis. Bill, this is Doug.

PHIL

So, I guess you have a pretty small penis.

CARL

Yeah, I guess so.

PHIL

Well, that's okay. I hear it doesn't really matter to women.

CARL

Yeah, I read that.

KEVIN

Okay you two, enough small penis talk!

DANA

Hey, Larry! Better put some sunblock on. The tip of your penis is getting real red!

VOICE

Thanks!

DENNIS

Hey, you guys want to see my pictures from Barbados? Okay, that's me and my Dad on a catamaran.

DANA

Penis looks great.

KEVIN

You've really got your Dad's penis.

***

Well, you get the idea. It went on that way for another five minutes, ending with a "campfire" song that probably will not made the *Hit Parade:*

> I once had a penis sing to me
> Penis penis song
> And when that penis penis sang

> Here was the penis song
> He'd sing to me
> Penis, penis, penis, penis, penis
> Penis, penis song
> Penis, penis, penis, penis
> Penis all day long
> Penis, penis, penis, penis, penis...

Hardly the satirical edge of a Jonathan Swift, and instantly rejected, but not without considerable debate. As differentiated from most, however, this one did not go away. The writer, a talented young man named Robert Smigel, was a chip off the Al Franken block — smart and relentless. And sincere in his belief that the piece was not obscene — that it made a valid satirical point. *SNL* had allowed the word by Franken and Davis in an anatomical context several years before, with minimal response, showing some progress from the era when the word "ass" could be used only in reference to the four-legged animal. Anyway, we argued and rewrote and compromised. We deleted one character and some of the cheapest vulgarities such as the sun block joke, generally tightened the dialogue and added an "advisory" at the end as Kevin stepped out of character to say,

> "Hi, I'm Kevin Nealon. What you just saw was an attempt to make an important point, that wherever you go, no matter how you look on the outside we we're all pretty much the same. You know, when the NBC Standards Department was dissolved, we welcomed it as an opportunity to deal with these issues in a frank way. To be honest with you, we're disheartened by the snickering we heard during this presentation. Kinda makes us wonder if there's room for serious discussion on these subjects on television. So, to those of you who missed the point...grow up. Really, come on."

The "Carl" in the script was actor Carl Weathers, but young Matthew Broderick was the host when the sketch was finally approved. He was persuaded into playing "Doug" and away we went! It was probably just as well that Carl Weathers did not participate. All we needed was adverse reaction to a black man in a cock routine.

We knew we'd hear from the public, and did we! The sketch generated 46,000 letters of complaint. 45,999 were form letters sent by Reverend Donald Wildmon and his American Family Association, the other one was from A.S.S., the Association of Stripped Sunbathers, complaining that we hadn't shown enough flesh! Just kidding.

In retrospect, doesn't the whole thing seem innocent and trivial in light of the Clarence Thomas hearings, the Lorena Bobbitt trial and the Starr Report? At the time, editorialists and columnists throughout the nation were unanimous in their approval of the use of "penis" in coverage of the Thomas hearings and Bobbitt trial. Columnist Ellen Goodman wrote, " I agree with anatomically correct speech. It would be absurd to speak of John Bobbitt's 'private parts,' let alone his 'peepee.' Anatomy isn't vulgarity." Or language maven William Safire in the *New York Times Magazine*, "Standard English has no dirty words. The word penis — severed or reattached, flaccid or erect — is as innocent, and usable in polite company."

As far as I was concerned, the vulgarity was not the use of the word in the Starr Report or the Bobbitt and Thomas situations, but in the press feeding frenzy over the cases. In his book, *Spread the Word* (Random House, 1999), Mr. Safire reprinted his original column along with a letter I'd sent in response to it:

"I thought you might be interested in a further history of 'penis' on television. I was the NBC censor on *Saturday Night Live*, a job most people believe doesn't even exist.

25

On December 15, 1979, Al Franken and Tom Davis used the word in a comedy routine that drew all of 24 negative telephone calls. But on October 15, 1988, we telecast a sketch called 'Nude Beach' in which the word was used about fifty times! In it, a bunch of nude guys, delicately covered by furniture, shrubbery, and even a guitar, gathered at a beachside bar and discussed their penises in a gossipy way, much as women might sit around yakking about hairdos. It was casual. conversational and matter-of-fact. Thus the word was spoken in a non-sexual, harmless, clinical way — which was the point of the sketch.

We debated hotly within the Broadcast Standards Department, finally deciding to consider the material less than tasteful, perhaps, but not obscene. And certainly within the parameters of *Saturday Night Live* acceptability at 11:30 PM.

Predictably, Reverend Donald Wildmon, the self-appointed guardian of America's morals, saw otherwise, as he generated a negative postcard campaign that eventually totaled over 46,000 pieces. Gosh, I wonder what he must be thinking as he watches the Bobbitt trial, the Thomas hearings, and the Buttafuoco/Amy Fisher confessions?

In any event, our friends at *Saturday Night Live*, always proud to be on the cutting edge of progressive humor, were once again a step ahead of popular opinion. And, while we had some monumental disagreements, I've always been comfortable with having approved 'Nude beach.'"

Obscenity is almost impossible to define although many have tried. The classic attempt was United States Supreme Court Justice Potter Stewart's "I can't define obscenity, but I know it when I see it." The FCC says, "Indecency: Language or material that depicts or describes in terms patently offensive as measured by contemporary community standards for the broadcast medium, sexual or excretory activities or organs." And NBC, without actually defining it, precludes it... "language and dialogue must be judged generally acceptable to a mass audience and appropriate to a public medium. Coarse or vulgar language should be avoided. Blasphemy and obscenity are unacceptable."

In 1973, the Supreme Court spelled out a three-part test of obscenity: If the "average person applying contemporary community standards" would find that, taken as a whole, the material appealed "to then prurient interest in sex," portrayed sexual conduct "in a patently offensive way" and lacked "serious literary, artistic, political or scientific value."

Oh, what muddy waters for a Broadcast Standards editor to cross! What are "contemporary community standards?" Which community? Los Angeles? Peoria? San Francisco? Perhaps we should merely follow the admonition of Judge Thomas J. Meskill of the United States Court of Appeals. Sustaining a lower court's ruling in 1983 that certain magazines and videos seized in Manhattan were not legally obscene, Judge Meskill reluctantly concluded that the "community standards in New York were so low that **nothing** was obscene."

And, oh yeah...what is an "average person?" No wonder standards editors get gray hair early.

Spoken obscenities were actually infrequent on *Saturday Night Live*, the most famous exception being Charlie Rocket's "fuck" on February 21, 1981. Charlie was playing J.R. Ewing in a parody of the "Who Shot J.R.?" episode of *Dallas*. At the close of the show, Charlie, still in character, was sitting onstage in a wheelchair saying goodnight with the rest of the cast. They were vamping to fill time and host Charlene Tilton asked Charlie how it felt to be shot. "I'd like to know who the fuck did it," he answered, smirking directly into the camera.

I'll never forget that moment. The control room went absolutely silent, then, as on swivels, every head turned to look at me! I saw this through my fingers, mind you, as my hands were covering my face, just before I beat my head against the console. "Thanks a lot, Charlie!" I groaned as I began to dial the telephone room to alert the staff to "Expect calls!" That was the night I set a personal best time between 8H and Engineering, only to find the tape editors had already deleted the vulgarity on the master tape for the West Coast feed. After all, we couldn't allow those sensitive folks in the west, especially those in Hollywood, to be exposed to such language! I wonder how the editors knew to expect me?

A few years later, a so-called comic, Martin Lawrence, hosted the show and used raunchy language in his monologue, including, according to the *New York Daily News*, "a string of jokes about feminine hygiene, oral sex and odd places to stick breath mints." All of this was unrehearsed and without the knowledge nor approval of the producer and director. What a jerk. It's unfortunate that no-talents like Lawrence can endanger an entire production (and network) with unprofessional antics.

I'm always surprised by the number of people who still assume that such escapades can be prevented, but *Saturday Night Live* is just that. Live. There is no seven-second delay nor pre-taping. What you see is what you get, warts and all, an actual happening in New York, although we were able to keep the airways pure for those sensitive folks in Hollywood and other points west who get the show on tape three hours later.

There were occasions when guest hosts ignored my requests to delete certain words, lines or bits of business. Lily Tomlin used to phrase "blow it out your arse" after she was told not to, Dennis Hopper gave the camera the finger and Howard Hesseman pretended to masturbate underneath the Update desk. Susan Saint James appeared once in a parody of her old TV series, *MacMillan and Wife*. The sketch had her rolling around under the covers in bed with someone assumed to be MacMillan but who turned out to be McDonald. Ronald, that is, as portrayed by funnyman Joe Piscopo. The problem was that she was obviously giving Ronald a blowjob under the sheets. After the dress rehearsal I passed word along to Susan that she should keep her head in plain sight, but on the air she took a dive anyway. Since she was dating the show's producer, Dick Ebersol (she would later marry him), there wasn't much I could say or do about it.

Once in a while, guests would throw in bits that we in Standards had no idea was coming. Those are the scariest moments you can have as a censor. One such instance involved David Bowie, who appeared as the show's musical guest in 1979, when he was in one of his weird costume periods. He came on wearing a bizarre pair of pants that swelled out to the sides in wide swoops, much like Munchkin bloomers. At the end of his number he struck a pose, staring off into space as the camera drew back. The audience applauded and the director prepared to dissolve to a commercial. What nobody but me seemed to notice was the mechanical penis that rose slowly and majestically from the folds of Bowie's pants! Fortunately, even in the control room this particular special effect was missed, and I didn't exactly call the *New York Times* to report the news. What I did was run for Engineering.

Such shenanigans on the part of performers on live television is unconscionable. Sinead O'Connor's behavior in ripping a picture of the pope was that of an undisciplined, unprofessional kook. Her actions, like that of Bowie, were unrehearsed and a surprise to the director, the producer, the writers and to Broadcast Standards. Such jerks, and I include those boobs who make political statements at the Academy Awards, have no class. They are entitled to their opinions. Their causes may be just. But there are proper avenues of debate and opinion — talk and interview shows specifically designed for such discussion — but awards and entertainment programs are not. Goodness, those people are pompous, pretentious — and boring.

It's no coincidence, I think, that the performers who were most pleasant to work with happened to be some of the biggest stars in the business. Robin Williams is a good example. To the audience, Williams' comedy seems improvised, pure stream of consciousness. In fact, he always knew, at least on *SNL*, exactly what he was going to say, and would make a point of checking

29

with me ahead of time if he felt any material might be edging over the line.

Don Rickles is another example of pure professionalism. I must admit I was nervous when Don was adlibbing his insults during his monologue but not once did he ever go too far. He was aware of the rules, and honored them. Even Eddie Murphy behaved himself. Despite his well-deserved reputation for lewdness (in his post-*SNL* career), and despite being something like 20 years-old when he was on the show, Eddie almost never said anything on the air that required bleeping. Joe Piscopo, on the other hand, seemed to slip in something bleepable almost every other week. It's a good thing that we didn't have to edit camera blocking and rehearsals, though!

By the way, Reverend Wildmon's 46,000 postcards campaign complaining about "Nude Beach" was far from the record. Audience Services counted 301, 204 postcards generated by the good Reverend in a pre-broadcast protest for the mini-series *Princess Daisy*. That's right, they were complaining even before they'd seen it! To put their protest in perspective, there were a grand total of just 31 viewer complaints following the telecast of *Princess Daisy*. Do you suppose that's all the people who were watching it?

Moral indignation is in most cases 2% moral, 48% indignation and 50% envy.
— **Vittorio DeSica**

In the twenty-five year history of *SNL*, there have been a host of hosts ranging from Catherine Oxenberg (who?) to Charlton Heston, from Joan Rivers to Rodney Dangerfield, from Nancy Kerrigan to Michael Jordan. Ratings have shown that, in general, male hosts are more successful than female and that Hollywood actors, used to a slower pace and innumerable retakes, are more likely to make scatalogical mistakes.

They all have one thing in common, however. They work like dogs for the week and are universally prepared to make fun of themselves. It was before my time, but Lorne Michaels is on record as claiming that the very worst host in the history of *SNL* was Milton Berle whose reputation for obnoxious behavior and bossiness was not diminished by his appearance, even though he was respected throughout the business as "Mister Television."

On the other hand, Sid Caesar, another television icon, turned out to be cooperative, gracious and giving, charming everyone with his personality and still-impressive talent. At the end of the show, the cast ensconsed him on a throne, dubbing him an honorary member of the "Not Ready for Prime Time Players", the only outsider ever so designated. It was a touching and well-deserved moment.

I can remember some duds. Robert Culp fancied himself a monologist and prepared his own opening remarks of numbing length and content. Mercifully, most were cut to make room for sketches and other funny stuff. When she took over for Lorne Michaels for one season, Producer Jean Doumanian asserted women's rights by booking such comic figures as Ellen Burstyn, Charlene Tilton, Karen Black, Sally Kellerman and Deborah Harry. Not a laugh in a carload.

Burt Reynolds never came up to his hype, although he had the courage to participate in what some critics considered the most tasteless sketch ever presented on *SNL*, "Vomitorium." I'm not sure there was a plot nor point to the sketch, it was a bunch of Roman guys in togas gorging themselves at a banquet, then tossing their cookies in troughs so they could go back to the bacchanal. I wish I had the script so I could recall why the heck we ever let it on the air.

On the other hand, there were groans when Angie Dickinson was booked, but by the time the show was over she'd delighted everyone with her personality, cooperation, hard work — and talent.

Buck Henry, Robin Williams and Tom Hanks have each hosted the show several times, but the all-time champion is Steve Martin whose comic style fit the *SNL* format perfectly. And what a professional! He showed his genius to me on two separate occasions. The first was on October 27, 1987, the night of the great NBC fire. Prior to our dress rehearsal, a fire broke out in an electric switching facility under 49th Street. Smoke billowed up into the street and filtered underground into the RCA building itself, necessitating evacuation of the building. The exodus by the *SNL* staff and crew from the 8th and 9th floors by stairway was uneventful, although some local WNBC news people were momentarily trapped on the 3rd floor.

The entire cast and crew of *SNL* repaired to Charley O's restaurant at the corner of 48th Street and Rockefeller Plaza where the network bought food and drink until such time as the Fire Department would allow us back into the studio. It was well after 9 PM when the all-clear sounded and we returned (some staggering back, courtesy of NBC's alcoholic largesse), too late for a full dress rehearsal. It would have been understandable if the show were cancelled as it promised to be a shambles. Even though a standby repeat show was in readiness in the videotape room, Lorne and Steve Martin courageously decided to continue. I'm convinced that Steve's calm demeanor and professional manner served to soothe the nerves of the entire assembly. The show was a bit rough but in my opinion, a triumph.

That situation was quite different from another show hosted by Steve, that of May 20, 1989. That was the very day we received the not unexpected but nevertheless shattering news that Gilda Radner had passed away from ovarian cancer. It is impossible to describe the grief and sense of loss in the *Saturday*

Night Live community. I'd known Gilda for only a season, but there were crew members who had known and loved her for four years. There were cast members who'd worked with her in Chicago and Toronto for many years, and, of course, Lorne, who'd discovered, nurtured and worshipped her. It was a devastating day, but in the finest tradition of "the show must go on", everyone donned their professional clothes and provided a superlative program.

The opening number was a wordless tribute — the videotape of a dance from the show of April 22, 1978. The setting was an elegant nightclub. Steve and Gilda, in true Astaire-Rogers tradition, spied each other across the dance floor, approached each other and, as everyone else froze, went into a torrid dance, twirling and sweeping across the floor. It was an amazing performance and a perfect tribute to one of the seminal stars of *Saturday Night Live.* How Steve Martin came back on stage to deliver his monologue after watching that tape, I'll never know. What I do know is that he's more than a superstar, he's a Super Star.

My fondest memories, of course, are of the regular cast members. I'm as star-struck as anyone else — well, perhaps a bit more jaded due to my celebrity associations in Hollywood. After all, it isn't everyone (excepting his wife and valet) who's seen a future President of the United States in his skivvies every week.

It was my personal policy, however, not to get too close to the cast or writing staff as we had to observe that invisible wall of impersonality. Not that they'd want me, anyway! Therefore I did not attend the weekly post-show parties held in a different gin mill, nor otherwise socialize, the only exception the year-end wingdings held for the show personnel and two or three thousand of Lorne's closest friends. That social extravaganza was normally held at the Rainbow Room of the RCA Building, or outdoors at the Rockefeller Plaza. But heck, it was NBC's money. What did Lorne care!

Even after the passage of twenty years or more, when folks find out my association with *SNL,* they invariably ask whether I knew John Belushi. I'd met him, but John had left the show by the time I arrived, well into his tragic descent into drug oblivion. What a waste. As were the premature deaths of other *SNL* stars; Gilda Radner from cancer; Phil Hartman, murder victim; Chris Farley, drug overdose; and Danitra Vance; breast cancer. For those who don't remember Danitra, she was a classically-trained Shakespearean actress/comedian who appeared during the 1985-1986 season. She was a delightful little African-American girl with a world of talent who rarely got a chance to show her ability. Like most women on *SNL*, she had to fight (and write) her way on to the show each week. I was not privy to such backstage maneuvering, but apparently it could be downright vicious.

In my tenure, the girls (Oops, I'm showing my age! Change 'girls' to 'women') had to follow television icons Gilda Radner, Jane Curtin and Laraine Newman, not an easy task. The original female writers responsible for much of the material tailored for the women had left by 1979, or were soon to leave — Rosie Shuster, Ann Beatts and Marilynn Miller were brilliant and hard to replace, therefore actresses Ann Risley, Gail Matthius, Christine Ebersole (Broadway star of *Camelot*!) and others suffered in comparison. Pam Stephenson, the English comedienne whose devastating impression of Margaret Thatcher never failed to break me up, was a fish out of water and returned to England a disappointed and more cynical talent. And who remembers that two-time Academy-Award nominee Joan Cusack spent a year with us. Or Tony Award nominee Denny Dillon spent a year being unappreciated for her wealth of talent, unfortunately not utilized.

The following year, under the supervision of producer Dick Ebersol, the writing and talent improved. I was very fond of Mary Gross whom I thought was an underrated talent. And the sweetest lady, I might add. Robin Duke had her moments, especially in "The Whiners" with Joe Picopo. Victoria Jackson, from the same era, was a delightful person with her squeaky voice, pretty much the real-life epitome of the ditsy blonde.

35

Victoria had a delightful six year-old daughter, Scarlet, whom she was always anxious to promote. One time, Victoria wrote a little piece about Scarlet's birth and asked me to review the videotape of some footage her husband had shot of Scarlet in the hospital soon after the delivery. Well, she hadn't spotted the tape properly and there I was, viewing the birth itself, with the camera on a tight closeup of Victoria's perineum with Scarlet's crown emerging! Vicki shrieked, "Oh, I guess I didn't rack this properly!" Since I'd brought up eight children, I assured her I'd pretty much seen it all, but she was embarrassed. According to *People Magazine,* Vicki has remarried, to a police officer, and is living happily in Florida. I hope so, for she's a sweet lady. The *People* article, from October 4, 1999, honored SNL's 25th Anniversary, with career updates on 75 performers who'd appeared on the show. I treasure it, for it put me back in touch with a lot of folks I respected and enjoyed. One of the regrets of the TV business is that associations are fleeting. When a show ends, the cast and production staff scatters to other ventures. Long-term friendships, therefore, suffer.

Victoria was part of the cast that included Jan Hooks and Nora Dunn. Now there was a pair! Their performance as the Sweeney Sisters, a brilliant satire on second-rate, gushy, insincere female singing duets was a killer. Jan was sort of the female Phil Hartman, who could do almost anything and do it well. Jan went on to success in Hollywood as a star of *Designing Women* and remains busy as a recurring character on *Third Rock from the Sun.* Nora was bit more cerebral — and a true female libber. She actually boycotted *SNL* one week, refusing to appear on the same program with host Andrew Dice Clay, protesting his attitude toward women. That took courage and a strong personal belief. I don't know if her stance helped or hurt her career. I hope not, for she's a terrific talent and a nice lady.

Then there's Julia Louis-Dreyfus who was wonderful on *SNL,* then went on to great fame as Elaine on *Seinfeld.* Julia and I shared the same birthday (Just a few years apart. Not.) I felt particularly close to her, and revel in her well-deserved success.

She arrived on *SNL* as part of a college comedy trio that included her future husband Brad Hall, and Gary Kroger. Brad often anchored News Update but I suspect he's more comfortable producing sitcoms in Hollywood than performing on camera. Gary Kroger brought a fresh-faced, all-American spirit to his comedy.

The guys had it a little easier as the writers somehow felt more comfortable writing for them. No one shall ever forget Eddie Murphy, Joe Piscopo, Billy Crystal and Martin Short. Their characterizations of Fernando, Gumby, Mr. Robinson and Ed Grimley were true television classics. Nor shall we ever forget Dana Carvey (The Church Lady and the quintessential George Bush), or the brilliant impressions of Phil Hartman (The heir to Dan Aykroyd who served as the 'glue' of the show.) Jon Lovitz, Master Thespian, The Liar and developer of other characterizations, was a lovely young man although his usual greeting became a bit tiresome, "Hey, Bill, can I say 'fuck' on the show this week?" Jon was the most modest performer I ever knew. He told me that before being chosen for *SNL,* he'd not made a dime in show business and never ceased being grateful at his good fortune which has continued post-*SNL*. I love his commercials as the man who invented the Yellow Pages.

Jim Belushi, John's brother, was on the show for awhile and did a great job although his talent was quite different from John's. To his credit, Jim was his own man, never trying to emulate his famous sibling. It's been heartwarming to observe Jim's success in motion pictures. Jim is a neat guy, and generous. I used to join Jim in his dressing room between dress and show for a chat and a beer. He chatted, I had the beer, to fortify myself for what was coming!

Another brother was Bill Murray's, Brian Doyle-Murray who never took advantage of, nor tried to imitate his sibling, but carved his own niche as a comic actor.

Then there were the humorists and commentators who sprinkled the show. Rich Hall, Dennis Miller and A. Whitney Brown were incisive, thoughtful observers of the world who added much to the humor of our times. The trouble they had on *SNL* was that their humor made a person **think**!

The most outstanding cast during my years was probably the one that included Billy Crystal and Martin Short. Lest we forget, it also included Michael McKean from *Laverne and Shirley,* Christopher Guest, and the outspoken Harry Shearer. Harry absolutely hated his association with the show and let everyone know it. But, my goodness, he was a bright and effective satirist. For example, he wrote and performed "South African Gold," (later) in my opinion one of the smartest sketches ever performed on the program. Unfortunately, he could be a real pain in the ass which hurt his chances of getting his stuff produced.

The 1980-1981 season was undoubtedly the least successful — only 13 shows were produced before the season was cut short and the show nearly terminated by NBC Management. While the show was poorly-received, not very funny and certainly tasteless, Producer Jean Doumanian, who had been promoted from Talent Coordinator, still had a very sharp eye for talent, however, bringing us Eddie Murphy, Joe Piscopo, Denny Dillon, Terry Sweeney and Gilbert Gottfried. Gilbert Gottfried perfected the shouting comedy later made famous by Sam Kinison. Gillie disappeared for awhile but seems to have found renewed success as a regular panelist on *Hollywood Squares.* Gillie, like Lovitz, always found it amusing to greet me with various manifestations of the f-word. I ran into him in Hollywood as late as 1996. He hadn't forgotten our greeting. Terry Sweeney, of course, was the first out-of-the-closet gay performer, whose in-drag impersonations of Nancy Reagan and Diana Ross were devastating.

Jean Doumanian's best friend was Woody Allen, and she spent many hours on the phone with him, even in the middle of rehearsals. Woody's advice and comic genius, however, could not save a floundering show careening out of control. While Jean Doumanian's name will always live in the infamy of *SNL*, we shall sponsor no benefits for her, as she is now the Executive Producer of each Woody Allen movie and still habituates

Elaine's and other glamour spots of Manhattan. In fairness, she stepped into a tough situation, following legend Lorne Michaels. She may not have been the answer to *SNL*, but she's a real talent and a nice lady.

Somehow the show survived (Of course it did, it was profitable!) Over the years we were delighted to welcome many personalities. One of my favorites was Randy Quaid, an actor I feel can do **anything**. After an unrecognizable stint on *SNL*, Randy went on to star as Lyndon B. Johnson in the TV mini-series, *LBJ*, played a cracker in the "Vacation" series with Chevy Chase, and now I hear him as the voice of Colonel Sanders in the KFC commercials. The man is talented!

Randy Quaid was in the mold of Dan Aykroyd, Phil Hartman, Kevin Nealon and Brian Doyle-Murray, those unsung "glues" that held the show together. Not necessarily "funny" per se, they were gifted comic actors off whom others played in the tradition of the great straight men of comedy — Bud Abbott, George Burns, Desi Arnaz and Dean Martin.

1980 also brought us two young talents, Anthony Michael Hall and Robert Downey, Junior. Hall was brought in following his success in *Seventeen Candles* and other teenaged flicks, but turned out to be a duck out of water. He disappeared from *SNL* without a ripple, reappearing not too long ago playing Bill Gates in *Pirates of Silicon Valley*. And brilliantly. I hope he makes a spectacular comeback. And what can one say about Robert Downey, Junior, who seems unable to extricate himself from the horror of drug addiction. Considering the brilliance of his motion picture performances, we can only pray that his career, not to mention his life, will fulfill its great promise.

We need not worry about Ben Stiller, David Spade and Rob Schneider (The Copy Room Guy) who are all brimming with Hollywood success. It is particularly pleasing to watch Ben as I'd attended Syracuse University with his dad, Jerry Stiller. As a matter of fact, I was Jerry's first straight man, in the musical *Girl Crazy*. We had a lot of fun, although he's had more success with his wife, Anne Meara, as his comedy partner.

39

A few years ago, I came out of retirement to set up a standards department for the WB Network and I enjoyed a visit with Rob Schneider and also reunioned with Garrett Morris who was guest-appearing on *The Wayans Brothers*. It had been a long road for Garrett, his life jeopardized by robbers who shot him in 1994, but he's made a full recovery with a career back on track.

Occasionally there were guest performers such as Andy Kaufman, a strange duck. Michael Davis, the comedy juggler, and illusionists Penn and Teller made their TV debuts on *SNL* (Penn joins Lovitz and Gottfried as an f-word aficianado) and the wonderful Harry Anderson (*Night Court*) was discovered on *SNL*. I remember I was called to Lorne's office to review a trick Harry wanted to do on the show, an illusion where it appeared he was sticking a big needle through his arm. I okayed it as a typical magic trick. It aired complaint-free, yet we caught hell for a different illusion wherein it appeared that Harry was eating a live hamster. I'm sure.

Speaking of motion pictures, which we weren't, it's incredible how many *SNL* performers have succeeded in films, starting with John Belushi, Chevy Chase and Dan Aykroyd. Bill Murray has had a great motion picture career, but who would have visualized the genius of Mike Myers? I loved Mike, probably because he was not only a fine young man, but he called me Mr. Clotworthy. It couldn't have been my reputation nor my vocation, it must have been my age! Mike was another of those wonderful Canadian talents and he was a joy to work with. And how can I not mention my favorite, Tim Kazurinsky? After all, he's the guy who impersonated me! Thankfully, he performed it rarely.

One performer who has been with the show longer than anyone else is announcer Don Pardo, the signature voice of the show. Dick Ebersol was a fine producer but he surely made a mistake when he replaced Don for a season. His replacement was a talented announcer, but just didn't have the pizzazz to deliver "It's Saturday Night Live!!!" like Pardo.

Don Pardo is one of NBC's senior staff announcers, associated with every game show and station break since the days of Marconi. Actually, it only seems that way, but he has been around. As have I which is perhaps why Don and I got along so well. And, speaking of age (make that experience) I can never forget my most gratifying relationship on *SNL*, that with Creative Consultant Herb Sargent, another gentleman of the old school. It is not true that Herb was a writer for Fatty Arbuckle, but he does go back a long time. Herb's baby each week was News Update. He prepared himself with an imitation of the Collier Brothers, cramming his office floor to ceiling with magazines and newspapers from around the nation. I wouldn't say his office was crowded, but it was put on high alert by the New York Fire Department. The result, however, was consistently sharp, incisive and funny material. Again, due to our age and experience, we became personally and professionally close, each keeping a jaundiced eye on the young whippersnappers putting this satirical show together. But no matter how slow the comedy week, or how untalented the host, Herb remained placid. After all, how could any temperamental actor bother a Marine veteran of Guadalcanal?

We had a string of Update anchormen and, while he'd never admit it, I suspect Herb's favorite (and certainly mine) was Dennis Miller. Dennis intimidated me a bit as he was so bright. He was (and is) much more than a standup comedian, he's an astute political commentator in the mold of Mark Russell and Mort Sahl. I just wish he'd get a haircut and clean up his language. You're brilliant, Dennis! You don't need the F-word! And you don't need the NFL gig, either.

The writers loved to play "Beat the Censor" once in a while. Tony Rosato (remember him?) and Christine Ebersole performed a sketch in 1981 called "Blackout" in which a couple returned home from grocery shopping during the New York blackout to find their curtains had fallen down. They tried to repair them in the dark, which led to "Grab hold of my rod," "Your melons are soft" and other such suggestive dialogue. Did we really let that go on?

But my favorite "Beat the Censor" piece was called "Fantasteecch Voyage" written by the talented (and weird) Andrew Smith. Andrew was totally outrageous, rarely getting a sketch past his own producer, much less Standards. But he had the funniest stuff in read-through! The premise of "Fantasteecch Voyage" was that actress Brooke Shields had slipped into a coma after "her appearance at the Grammy Awards." To save her life, a team of doctors was placed in a submarine, all shrunk to microscopic size and injected into her bloodstream. Dare I continue?

CAPTAIN

Up periscope.

JOE

Down periscope.

CAPTAIN

Up periscope.

JOE

Down periscope.

GARY

Stop! Captain, are you crazy? Up and down, up and down…

CAPTAIN

We were injected into Brooke Shield's thigh, weren't we?

Well, I like that girl. I saw *Blue Lagoon* five times.

JOE

Up periscope.

GARY

Captain, she's only a freshman...

JOE

Okay, okay...the periscope is up. It's going to stay up. I won't even touch it. Let's take a look, What's our position?

JIM

Thirty three degrees north, fifteen degrees west.

JOE

Depth?

JIM

Six inches.

JOE

But where the hell are we?

JIM

It's like the Bermuda Triangle, Captain...You know what I mean?

JOE

You mean that place where seamen are lost without a trace and compasses go kaplooey?

JIM

Yeah, and the weather is real <u>foul</u>. Know what I mean?

JOE

But wait, this isn't the Atlantic Ocean, this is Brooke Shields.

William G. Clotworthy

SUDDENLY THERE IS A COLLISION, THERE IS THE SOUND OF SCRAPING ALONG THE HULL

BRAD
What the hell was that? A depth charge?

JOE
Close, Ensign. Down here it's called an I.U.D. It could have been curtains if we'd been out there alone, but this baby can get through anything..."

The voyage went on ad nauseum as the crew entered Brooke's brain (where they found nothing but a desert) before emptying their garbage and port-o-sans in her brain before exiting at the Bermuda Triangle.

Well, it got some embarrassed giggles from the women at read-through.

Offstage, the wildest cast member I had to deal with was probably Bill Murray. I can tell you that Billy's reputation as a lunatic was completely justified. A charming lunatic most of the time, but definitely off the wall. I remember running into him at a wrap party at the end of the 1980 season. I had my wife in tow and we happened to be celebrating our wedding anniversary. It was a mistake mentioning this to Billy who was, to put it delicately, drunk off his ass. He let out an earsplitting congratulatory whoop, picked up my wife — literally — and planted a very wet, very tonguey kiss directly on her mouth. Scared her half to death — she'd never met the guy before.

Another, sadder occasion in which Billy struck me as being somewhat out of control was at the memorial service for Gilda. Lorne put together a private, invitation-only gathering in 8H for a hundred or so people who'd worked with Gilda over the years. It was an emotional affair. A number of people — Lorne and director Dave Wilson were two I remember — gave funny, touching recollections of the woman we'd all loved. Billy's comments were neither funny nor touching. He got up near the

44

end and launched into a passionate, disjointed diatribe about how Gene Wilder, Gilda's husband, had taken Gilda away from the people who knew and loved her best, that she'd been separated from her true friends and true work. The implication was that Wilder had somehow been responsible for Gilda's death! I was stunned. Just as stunning was the reaction of the other people. Most seemed to feel that Billy had gone a little too far, but that the gist of what he was saying was true. Gene Wilder, needless to say, was not in attendance.

In Billy's defense, I think he was torn up about Gilda's death — the two of them has been romantically involved at one time. In any event, it was the only instance I can remember where Bill Murray seemed to have a mean-spirited bone in his body.

Though my wife was unhappy with my erratic hours and jealous of the demands of the entertainment business, she, like most, was star-struck. She didn't much care for Bill Murray's french kiss, but loved the parties and fine dining whenever we went on the town (i.e., on the expense account) entertaining an important client in town. One evening we were wining and dining a client at an "in" Hollywood bistro when a party of four was seated at the next table, the four being Robert Wagner, Natalie Wood, Steve McQueen and Ali McGraw! Angela hardly ate a bite. Whenever she turned her head to stare at the stars, she stuck her fork in her cheek!

As we left, I made a pit stop and who should wander in to stand at the next urinal but Wagner. I was just dizzy enough to say hello and make a comment that we had something in common; we were both married to beautiful women of Russian ancestry. He was properly polite, we washed up, and left the men's room together. Angela was standing with her back to us as I went up and said, "Oh, Angie, I'd like you to meet Robert Wagner!" She turned, mouth agape. Wagner, in his most charming manner, made an appropriate remark although nonplussed by this staring, stupidly silent woman. Or perhaps she was going "Gggggggghhh." There she was, meeting one of Hollywood's most glamorous leading men, frozen in embarrassment, unable to speak — and absolutely pissed at me for not giving her fair warning!

Anyone who willingly takes the job of censor tends to
be, shall we say, not very smart.
— **Tom Shales**, TV critic

In addition to all the corporate sturm und drang that resulted from Charlie Rocket's indiscretion, it prompted the first communication between NBC and the aforementioned Reverend Donald Wildmon of Tupelo, Mississippi. Reverend Wildmon has worn several cloaks of respectability, at that time representing the American Family Association that described itself as "a Christian organization promoting the Biblical ethic of decency in American society with primary emphasis on TV and other media." After Charlie's goof, Wildmon called the Audience Services Department first thing Monday morning, not only to object to "fuck," but to demand that Rocket be fired and, further, that NBC issue an apology. Audience Services is well-trained in fielding complaints but their assurances to Wildmon that the word was unscripted and inadvertent fell on deaf (read "closed") ears. According to the Audience Services report, Wildmon said, "We've laid off NBC. Your profits have been 50% lower than three years ago, but if Charles Rocket is not fired, we'll cost you a chunk of money and we can do it. If Rocket is on again next Saturday, we'll see to it that as much advertising as possible will be lost."

Subsequent memos show that Wildmon continued to call almost daily with more threats and when Charlie was not fired as demanded, he carried his campaign directly to the advertising community. This was only the first of many threats Wildmon would issue. In my experience, none of them had much of an effect. No, my problem with Wildmon was that I quite often agreed with him! And with Newton Minow who, many years before, had referred to TV as a "vast wasteland." Unfortunately, we had to work within the system, as juvenile and dumb and crazy as it might be. It was Wildmon's tactics and bullying nature that made him dangerous. Here's an example:

TO: CEOs OF COMPANIES ADVERTISING ON
      TELEVISION
RE: NBC-TV'S USE OF VULGARITY

On Saturday Night Live (February 21, 1981) Charley Rocket, a star of the program, had the following to say in answer to a question.

"Aw, man, I feel lousy. This is the first time I have ever been shot in my life. I would like to know who the fuck did it."

We asked NBC to dismiss Mr. Rocket from the program in order to make sure that this offensive remark was not repeated. Instead NBC simply issued the following:

"It was an unintended and inexcusable remark. NBC apologizes for offending any viewers."

In addition, we have learned that just prior to that episode NBC had a very lengthy debate over whether to allow the use of the term "cunt" on one of their programs.

In light of the above, and because NBC refused to take proper disciplinary action, NBC WILL BE SCORED DOUBLE IN OUR MONITORING REPORT DURING MARCH, APRIL AND MAY. In other words, each score for violence, sex and profanity will be doubled for those advertisers sponsoring NBC programs. If a program normally would score 10, then if it is an NBC program, that score will be 20.

This type of language will not be condoned or accepted. It is regrettable that NBC listens only to the language of money. But if that is the language to be used, we plan to use it.

In selecting the company to ask for a one year boycott of all their products, you need to remember that each score you receive for sex, violence and profanity on NBC will be doubled.

Also, enclosed you will find additional groups which have joined the coalition. If you have any questions, please feel free to contact us.

Sincerely,

Donald E. Wildmon
Chairman, Coalition for Better Television

Charlie Rocket was not on my short list of favorite performers and I've always been miffed that he never had the courtesy to apologize personally — after all, I took a lot of the heat! But I was willing to forgive his transgression as an unfortunate mistake. And he did catch hell. NBC Management, led by the Law Department, put producer Jean Doumanian and the entire cast on warning and Charlie sent a note to Brandon Tartikoff, President of NBC Entertainment, apologizing for his indiscretion, claiming it was not premeditated... "fully aware that if it happens again the consequences would be most serious. I have already promised myself it would not happen again. I extend the same promise to you. I hope you rest assured."

Well, Charlie was assured, the network was assured and even I was assured. But not Reverend Wildmon who, petty and vengeful, kept up the pressure to terminate an actor who'd made a mistake. What's the matter, Rev? Didn't they teach you the Golden Rule at the Seminary? And where, oh where did he get the information about using the word "cunt?" That was an outrageous and unconscionable statement, patently untrue.

Wildmon, of course, was only the latest in a long string of do-good politicians, preachers and others sincerely concerned about the effect of television on the national psyche or, more likely, the positive effect of their negativity on their own careers. For example, the National Coalition for Decency attacked the networks for being too sexy in their programming. Breathing brimstone and threatening boycotts a la Wildmon, the preachers demanded that TV clean up its act — or else. In most cases their causes are narrow; stereotypical depictions of their ethnic group and the like — and opinions differ on their importance and impact on public perception, governmental regulation and industry action.

Some years ago NBC conducted a comprehensive survey of the most important pressure groups; their financial stability, their stated purpose, staff personality, interaction with other groups, and perceived influence. The study began with a detailed questionnaire, ending with lengthy interviews conducted by telephone or in person. NBC was anxious to update its relationship with the Special Interest Groups; to study their aims and activities and, in particular, to interface with groups concerned with television; groups that were national in scope, broad in membership, and operated in Washington, DC.

NBC's consultant was asked to determine many factors. Were the group leaders upset about television? Did their own television image still bother them? How did they feel about the prevailing climate as regards sex, violence, language? Were they planning any overt action such as boycotts, demonstrations, mailings or protests? Were they part of a coalition?

The findings were surprising, and fascinating. The leaders, pleased to be asked, were brutally honest. Many were upset with NBC, some saddened at the networks' seeming lack of interest in their agenda; others concerned about GE's purchase of NBC and what they perceived as an abandonment of the philosophy of public interest with substitution of only bottom line aims. Most assumed that NBC was willing to live with the heat engendered by that philosophy and consequently, interest groups were being forced to turn to advertisers and Congress for a hearing. Most had engaged in some anti-network advocacy either individually or in coalition, i.e., testifying for various bills, lobbying the FCC, supporting reinstitution of the Fairness Doctrine and the Children's TV Act, and working to influence congressmen or their aides.

There was almost universal disapproval of Reverend Wildmon and his tactics. "We'll never come on like Wildmon, who is wrong in almost everything he does...However, I don't think the networks have been very intelligent in handling him. This one little twit down in Mississippi is winning the media battle despite the fact no one supports him and the public at large disagrees with his kind of censorship" — "the sledgehammer approach of Wildmon et al has a definite political agenda — it is political blackmail" — "he gets the most response — his complaints hit every single TV show with their anti-Christian conspiracy" — "he may be better at external communications than the networks are, at least in terms of image. There are a lot of groups dissatisfied with TV, but who really believes that TV is anti-Christian? Yet he's making inroads and the networks are standing by. I think the networks are like carpenters who never fix their own steps. You communicate brilliantly for everyone but yourselves." — "It's no wonder Wildmon is riding high as he is. Most of us laugh at this little creep and we know his boycotts are ludicrous. But I'll bet he's cost you plenty — at least in time and reputation which is money. He had a mimeo machine in his garage and today the SOB has more computers than IBM. You did that. You've made this idiot what he is today — rich."

Well, no one, except the networks themselves, ever said TV executives were bright. How else can one explain *Waverly Wonders* and *South of Sunset*?

Whom the Gods would make bigots
They first deprive of humour.
— James M. Gillis

In their anger over *Saturday Night Live*, gay and lesbian groups shared much in common with Reverend Wildmon, although they tended to be more pleasant to deal with. Of all the sketches I approved during my tenure, one I regret most was a smarmy little number called "Two Guys." It portrayed a gay man, played by host Steve Guttenberg, trying various ruses to get a blind man, played by Jon Lovitz, into bed. As any number of angry gays pointed out, the sketch reinforced the myth that homosexuals somehow need to trick unsuspecting straights into having sex. It didn't exactly offer a sensitive picture of sightless people, either.

One sketch we didn't approve that maybe we could have was "Scared Straight," a parody of the documentary film of the same name, the one that showed seasoned convicts scaring young offenders by telling them graphic stories about how awful prison life can be. In *SNL*'s version, two teenagers considering going gay are taken to a cocktail party at an interior decorator's house in the Hamptons where they witness the "horror" of the gay lifestyle first hand. The host makes catty remarks about his guests' clothes and hair styles; the conversation is about fashion designers or Bette Midler movies, and jaded queens lead innocent young men into a back room for "brunch."

OPEN ON GIL AND ROBERT AS STREET KIDS
ADMIRING A POSTER FOR A GAY PORNO FLICK.
JOE ENTERS

JOE (Menacingly)
Thinking of turning gay, boys?

GIL (Surprised)
No, we were just looking.

JOE
You young punks! You say to yourselves, "Sure, I'm <u>gay</u>. I don't care. They don't enforce those laws

against <u>homosexuals</u>..." Well, we'll just see how cocky you are <u>after</u> this weekend. We're going to send you to the Big House until you're (LOOKS DIRECTLY INTO CAMERA) Scared Straight!

(TITLE SLIDE: SCARED STRAIGHT) (MUSIC:SCARY DOCUMENTARY MUSIC)

CUT TO INTERIOR OF FANCY HAMPTON HOUSE. WELL-DRESSED. WELL-GROOMED MEN ARE STANDING AROUND CHATTING. JOE LEADS GIL AND ROBERT IN.

JOE

You're stuck here at this big house party for the weekend.

(CHYRON: "SIMULATED 'GAY' PARTY")

ROBERT

Big deal.

JOE

You think a house party's a lot of fun, don't you? Well, take a look at our "guests." (CHYRON: "POLICE DECOYS") Catty, vicious, bored to tears. Just waiting to dish you the filth.

CHARLIE (Insidious)

Come on in, boys. All right, the game is charades. You in the tacky jacket, you're first.

GIL IS PUSHED INTO THE MIDDLE OF A CIRCLE OF PARTY GUESTS WHO ARE ALL SCREAMING

GUESTS

How many words? Book or movie? First letter? Sounds like?

> GIL (Hysterical and flustered)
> I can't think of anything!

> JOE (Bitchily mocking him)
> I can't think of anything!!! Oh, get over it, Mary. Next!

This sort of thing went on for awhile including cocktail hour conversation about the latest Bette Midler film and the late Judy Garland. Gil was led to another room for "brunch" which led to this ending:

> FRENCH DOORS OPEN AND CATATONIC GIL IS LED IN

> GIL
> Bring on the girls! I want a woman! Get me a date!

> CHARLIE
> We still have plenty of quiche. Anyone else for "brunch?"
> JOE AND CHARLIE PUSH ROBERT TO FRENCH DOORS
> We're pretty tough on them, but someday they'll thank us.

> JOE
> For being (TURNS TO CAMERA) Scared Straight.

***

From one perspective, the sketch was an hilarious, knowing spoof of gay stereotypes, as well it might have been since one of its writers was Terry Sweeney, the only overtly gay writer-performer ever on *Saturday Night Live*. Whether the homophobes in the audience would understand that this was a

56

parody was something else entirely. Making fun of stereotypes on television is a very ticklish business. In order to satirize prejudice, you must show prejudice, and not everybody will recognize it as satire. The fact that Terry Sweeney was gay didn't change the potential danger of putting "Scared Straight" on the air. Countless times a writer would claim that making fun of a certain minority group was okay because the writer was a member of that group and therefore knew better than the censors, what would or wouldn't offend other members of that group. "Al's Jewish!" the refrain went, or "Eddie's black!" The arguments carried some weight, but not much. Anybody who claims that Eddie Murphy's perspective is shared by all blacks, or that Al Franken is representative of all Jews is simply wrong. Same with "Scared Straight." Terry and his co-writer, Pam Norris, tried for weeks to come up with an acceptable (to us) version of the piece but never succeeded.

I often wondered how some of the gay activists would have reacted if they'd seen the stand-up routine Eddie Murphy and Joe Piscopo performed to warm up the live audience in Studio 8H. They played Laurel and Hardy as gays, very horny gays. This routine wasn't really any of my business since it wasn't going out on the air, but I found it embarrassing that members of the studio audience — guests of NBC, many of them teenagers — were subjected to something so raunchy. My boss wrote a letter to the programming executive in charge of the show, trying delicately to explain the problem, but some things don't translate very well into corporatese:

> "It has been reported that the actors who performed the warmup for this Saturday's *SNL* used extremely coarse language and questionable physical actions. This has occurred in the past. On those occasions (*SNL* Producer) Dick Ebersol was asked to make clear to the performers that company policy does not allow such behavior in front of an audience. We do allow greater leeway to *Saturday Night Live*, but cannot accept or

condone the use of such words like: 'm.....f.....,' 'f......a......,'b...-f......' or physical actions which portray the latter."

The memo did not work and Eddie and Joe's b...-f...... routine continued.

Stereotyping is a very delicate subject, especially in a satirical show, as satire is a fragile comedic device, easily misunderstood and often resented — especially if you're the butt of the joke. Or not. For example, we once approved a parody commercial that I considered a brilliant swipe at South African apartheid, but it used one word offensive to African-Americans, hence it was a tough call. But the satirical point was honest and made the language not only viable, but absolutely essential.

SOUTH AFRICAN GOLD

(SLIDE: A ROLLER COASTER LABELED 'STOCK MARKET')

HARRY (VO)
The stock market rises and falls...
(SLIDE: A WAD OF DOLLARS)
Savings account interest doesn't even keep up with inflation.
(SLIDE: AN ALBUM FULL OF STAMPS)
And stamps take years to collect.
CUT TO HARRY SEATED IN A DEN, DRESSED IN BUSINESS SUIT

HARRY
Now, for those who are smart enough to recognize the world's finest investment, and secure enough not to have to apologize for it, the South African Gold Board introduces a distinguished new gold coin...(PICKS UP

DISPLAY CASE CONTAINING A GOLD COIN. WE CANNOT SEE DETAILS ON COIN)

...the Niggerand. This one-ounce, 99.9 percent fine gold coin commemorates the labor of those who made it possible...

CUT TO CLOSEUP OF COIN SHOWING ON THE FRONT SIDE A FINE GOLD COIN HEAD AND SHOULDERS SCULPTURE OF A BLACK MAN

...a beautifully etched portrait of an actual African minesman. On the reverse...

CUT TO BACK OF COIN, A MAP OF SOUTH AFRICA

...a beautifully etched map of the areas where, by law, these workers are allowed to live.

CUT BACK TO HARRY

You'll want to treasure your Niggerands for years to come — or you'll want them for a special person on your gift list. Nothing expresses your feelings of caring better than a Niggerand — it's the gift that keeps on grinning. So now is the perfect time to begin your investment program.

CUT TO FRONT OF COIN

HARRY (VO)

Visit your selected bank or brokerage house and put your future in Niggerands — because even the color blind can see gold.

***

A few years ago the late and brilliant Chicago writer Mike Royko wrote a column, "Time to be Colorblind to all Words of Hatred," based on an imbroglio in Sacramento, California. Following a speech by Reverend Louis Farrakhan, editorial cartoonist Dennis Renault of the *Sacramento Bee,* executed a panel showing hooded Ku Klux Klan members looking at a copy of Farrakhan's speech. One of the boys is saying, "That nigger makes a lot of sense."

Appropriate. To the point. Sharply satirical. Contextually proper.

And manically criticized, just as we were for "South African Gold." *The Sacramento Bee* was inundated with protests and demands for an apology, even Renault's head on a platter. The protests, mind you, did not come from the KKK whose ignorant prejudices had been ridiculed, or even from the Reverend Farrakhan whose outrageous diatribes prompted the cartoon. No, they came from the black community, enraged by the use of the word "nigger." Even though the cartoonist was clearly sympathetic to black sensitivities, the satirical thrust flew right by, prompting Royko to comment, "…in doing so, they made his point. If he offended them while doing a cartoon sympathetic to their cause—the fight against bigotry—then what does that say about Farrakhan's chronic Jew baiting and white baiting? If one word, used in sympathy to their social causes, could enrage them, then how do they think Catholics or Poles feel about the first Polish pope being described by Farrakhan's chum as 'the old, no-good pope, you know, that cracker.'"

Regretfully, the *Sacramento Bee* collapsed in the face of the misguided protests and apologized in a front-page editorial. NBC did not apologize for "South African Gold," although brought to task by many black leaders including Manhattan Borough President Percy Sutton.

Context and intent are essential in making decisions on such material and it seems to me that considering any word so offensive that it should never be used is self-defeating. Ironically, those who screamed the loudest about "nigger" were strangely silent when Eddie Murphy performed his most insulting and stereotypical characters — the black pimp Velvet Jones or the sleazebag Mr. Robinson. Could it be that those characters were so funny that they were exempt from criticism, with no satirical bite?

African-Americans, of course, were not the only ethnic group to bitch about *SNL*. After all, we called the program NBC's Equal Opportunity Offender and we heard from just about all of them, some with complaints unknown to us as offensive. As a World War II veteran, I didn't think much about a wartime sketch in which some marines in battle referred to the enemy as "Japs." After all, for years we'd had the "Yellow Peril" and "Slant-Eyes" and the like. But then Joe Picopo did a brilliant impersonation of Frank Sinatra (hardly Mr. Taste) in a spoof of his then-current Chrysler commercials that pushed the sale of American cars. In the satire, Sinatra referred to "Japs" and the sushi hit the fan! "Deeply offended by your lack of sensitivity in denigrating people of Japanese ancestry" — "hostile attack on Japanese people in general" — "use of term 'Japs' is a constant reminder of the days Japanese-Americans spent in the concentration camps during World War II" — "This segment has caused consternation, hurt and anger in many quarters of the Japanese-American community."

On one hand I wanted to shout, "Who the hell won the war?!!" but common sense prevailed and we realized we were being provided a valuable lesson in forgiveness, understanding and genuine tolerance.

On the other hand, how does one reply to this letter?

> "I was surprised to see *Saturday Night Live* air 'Great Moments in the History of White Trash.' I am of the white race and I take this as a racial slur. I deeply resent it. Therefore I am now an ex-NBC booster. From now on I'll turn my TV to another station."

What that writer needs, obviously, is a Special Interest Group. Everybody else has one. How about NEWT (Non-Educated White Trash?)

Here's a partial list of groups with whom we worked (or fought with) over the years:

Action for Children's Television
Accuracy in Media
AFL-CIO
American-Arab Anti-Discrimination Committee
AARP
American Coalition of Citizens with Disabilities
Americans for Responsible Television
American Humane Association
American Jewish Committee
American Legion
American Library Association
American Medical Association
Anti-Defamation League of B'nai B'rith
Association of Franco-Americans
Black Citizens for a Fair Media
Boy Scouts of America
California Governor's Committee for Employment of the Handicapped
Center for Study of Responsive Law
Church of Jesus Christ of Latter-Day Saints
CLEAR-TV
Common Cause
Elks
Gray Panthers
Interfaith Center on Corporate Responsibility
International Association of Machinists
International Gypsy Commission
INFACT
Japanese American Citizens League
Knights of Columbus
League of United Latin American Citizens (LULAC)
League of Women Voters
Media Institute
Mexican-American Legal Defense and Educational Fund
Moral Majority
Morality in Media

NAACP
National Action Forum for Older Women
National Asian American Telecommunications Committee
National Association of Evangelicals
National Alliance for the Mentally Ill
National Association of Attorneys General
National Black Media Coalition
National Citizens' Committee for Broadcasting
National Coalition of Hispanic Human Services Organizations
National Coalition on TV Violence
National Commission on Working Women
National Congress of American Indians
National Council of the Churches of Christ
National Council of La Raza
National Council of Negro Women
National Council of Senior Citizens
National Education Association
National Federation for Decency
National Gay and Lesbian Task Force
National Italian-American Foundation
National Organization of Women
National Puerto Rican Forum
National Religious Broadcasters
National Rifle Association
National Urban League
NOSOSTROS
Nurses Media Watch
Organization Against Sexism and Institutional Stereotypes (OASIS)
Older Women's League
Organization of Chinese-Americans
People for the American Way
Parents Music Resource Center
Planned Parenthood
Polish-American Congress

Polish-American Guardian Society
Pro-Life Action League
PTA
Rural American Women
Screen Actors Guild
Slavic American National Association
Sons of Italy
Southern Baptists Convention
Telecommunications Research and Action enter
US Catholic Conference
UNICO
United Methodist Church
Women Against Violence
Women's Action Alliance
YMCA
YWCA

One of the most difficult Special Interest Groups with whom to work was the Arab-American Anti-Discrimination Committee. In the first place, none of us were familiar with the Muslim religion and, second, for quite some time the United States had been in confrontation with Muslims, whether it be the Ayatollah, Qadaffi or splinter terrorist groups responsible for blowing up buildings or hijacking aircraft and pleasure ships. We had to exercise extreme care in dramatic presentations to ensure that the Muslim religion wasn't being defamed; that comedy didn't insult basic beliefs and tenets. For example, when a wealthy sheik decorated the exterior of his Beverly Hills mansion with nude statuary featuring painted-on pubic hair, that was acceptable fodder for the satirist, but referring to him as a "rag head" would be a no-no as the Muslim headgear had religious significance.

In an uncomfortable situation reminiscent of Daniel entering the lion's den, my superiors "volunteered" my appearance at a national convention of the Anti-Discrimination Committee.

NBC's religious advisor, Doctor Richard Gilbert, helped me with my speech. Helped? Heck, he wrote it:

> "It's a real pleasure to be here, although I accepted your invitation with trepidation, After all, what am I, the quintessential WASP, doing here? I suspect NBC sent me here very much as Leo II (718) of Constantinople sent envoys to the Caliph Omar II of the victorious Muslim armies asking what he had in mind? Further perspective prompts me to say that while my Anglo-Saxon ancestors were living in trees and painting themselves blue, your ancestors were inventing the zero, building exquisite mosques and writing profound theologies. Nothing can dilute our respect for your rich heritage.
>
> My chief qualification for being on this panel is my responsibility as Broadcast Standards editor on the most outrageous show on network television — *Saturday Night Live.* We call it our Equal Opportunity Offender. I can't think of any individual from Qadaffi to Arafat to Reagan to any ethnic or religious group that hasn't been insulted by the program. All in the cloak of comedy and satire, of course.
>
> We've even managed to offend multiple groups in a single sketch. During the 1984 election campaign, Jesse Jackson referred to New York as 'Hymietown.' Shortly after, Eddie Murphy impersonated Jackson and sang to Jews in wah-wah soul music:

> 'Don't let me down, Hymietown.
> We blacks feel close to all you Hymies and Hymettes,
> We have so much in common
> Because we've both been oppressed
> We both have big noses

> And gold chains on our chests.
> You know I love the black suits you wear
> And the little black curls
> Don't let me down, Hymietown.'

I don't remember whether we got more complaints from Blacks for ridiculing Jackson, or from Jews for stereotyping. Nobody was amused. Except the audience.

Of course, that's exactly the problem we're faced with in Broadcast Standards: Can you offend minorities in order to entertain majorities? We're all concerned about hurting the few while amusing the many — our toughest job to balance the interests of the viewers in whose homes TV is a guest, against the needs and desires of the creative community for freedom of expression — all in the context of the American diversity of taste and values.

Most of the programs you see on network television are made by independent producers, from whom the network rents the shows. Producers own the shows, the networks do not. Normally the networks have the right to a single airing plus one rerun before the rights revert to the producer who is free to re-rent the show to a syndicator — which is why you still see *MASH, Mary Tyler Moore, I Love Lucy* and the others on local stations over and over.

Now, if you're an independent producer, what is your aim? Is it the public interest, or to interest the public? Is it to avoid controversy or stereotyping and ethnic slurs, or is it grabbing audiences?

Let's face it, the producer is a story-teller, not the guardian of the nation's morals. And stories, now and forever, need heroes, conflict, and villains. Over the years we've told producers that they cannot villainize Protestants, Catholics, Jews, Blacks, Puerto Ricans, Mexicans, Italians, Poles, Chinese, Japanese, Gays,

Aged, the Disabled, Veterans, Workers, Business Executives, Southern Sheriffs, Mad Scientists, Women…well, you get the idea.

About the only villains left are your people and mine, middle-class Anglo-Saxons and Arabs. And it looks like, and I hail this development, we may be running out of Arab bashing, in no small measure due to your efforts. For how do we learn about negative stereotyping and those they offend? Sometimes we hear from the general public, but more often than not from the 125 or so Special Interest Groups with agendas not unlike yours. And over the past few years NBC has held five national seminars with the major racial, religious, ethnic, educational and minority groups — what some have called our natural enemies. The groups teach us about their sensitivities, and we try to show them what it's like to tell stories to a nation where almost anything you say is going to offend someone. (Ed. note: This was before NBC's "downsizing." Such seminars are a long-lost vestige of a company's once-noble attempt to do right by everyone.)

Fortunately, there are a few talented writers who can both interest the public and serve the public interest at the same time. TV has produced some very positive black images, and I look forward to the time when we can see dramas which pick up the heartbreak of anti-semitism aimed at Arab-Americans or a *Movie of the Week* that shows the Palestinian agony from the perspective of a Palestinian.

Meanwhile, I attempt to evaluate each script on its merits, paying attention to the interest it generates, the genre it represents, to the audience its aimed at, and, finally, the values or disvalues it incorporates. In other words, I sit in for the average reasonable viewer. Hey, it's not all bad. I have to review every bathing suit and shower scene, and every pajama party romp. It's a tough job, but someone's got to do it.

We are all imperfect people living in an imperfect world, but I assure you of our sincere desire to understand you and your history, culture, religion and heritage. NBC is not in business to offend viewers. You are important to us and that's why I'm happy to be here — to listen, to learn, and to communicate."

I hate to admit it, but I had the feeling my audience wasn't particularly moved by my oration. But we sure tried to accommodate everyone, though it wasn't always easy. But here's what we tried to do for the Arab-American community one time:

NBC purchased a successful feature film, *Protocol,*starring Goldie Hawn as a Washington secretary who saves the life of a visiting Arab dignitary. In gratitude, he wants to marry her. The film took a comedic look at Muslim attitudes towards women and, appallingly, made a womanizing, alcohol-guzzling caricature of the sheik's religious advisor! The Arab-American community was rightfully angered by the film at the time of its original release and strenuously reiterated those objections to us. With script in hand and with the assistance of skilled editors at Warner Brothers, I looked at the picture many times, keeping in mind those complaints. The film was re-cut, voice-overs added, and dialogue dubbed that actually changed the character of the religious advisor to a "fortune-teller." It's amazing what one can do in an editing room to assuage the feelings of a Special Interest Group, retain the entertainment value, and, not incidentally, save your company's financial investment.

Sometimes nothing helps, witness a Burt Reynolds classic, *The End*. In the film, comedian Dom DeLuise portrayed a Polish schizophrenic, a performance highlighted by a series of vulgar Polish jokes — "You don't sing the Polish national anthem, you fart it," and others equally gross. The Polish Special Interest Groups made lots of noise of protest, all of it unnecessary as we also considered the humor offensive and unacceptable and had already removed the Polish jokes. In rare recognition of our efforts, we received letters of commendation from several Polish-American groups: "We would like to express our appreciation for the care and diligence taken by NBC to extract all the material offensive to us..." or "...I know that all our members appreciate the concerns that you have shown us."

Nice, huh? Well, not to one Polish-American group... "despite NBC's efforts to clean up the motion picture presentation, we continue to question the overall worthiness of this film, based on its knowing history, for network showing, and further feel that renewed showings of this film, based again on its original reputation, can only foster a continuing anti-Polish bigotry, even though it might come in a more cleaned-up package."

In other words (I think), they are saying that the folks who saw the film in theatrical release are disposed to remember what the group perceives as anti-Polish bias and stereotyping when they see it on TV years later? Even though the offensive material had been excised?

Ah, you can't win in Broadcast Standards.

What did Shakespeare say about the "eye of the beholder?" Two of the most popular characters ever on *SNL* were the Festrunk Brothers, the Czech immigrants portrayed by Steve Martin and Dan Aykroyd. NBC and the majority of the audience loved them. Well, most of the audience did, with at least one exception:

> "...we, Americans of the Czechoslovak origin, were very displeased and insulted by the presentation of two men as being refugees from Czechoslovakia. These individuals were two characters of a very low capability, skill and moral values. They did not know how to dress properly and how to behave. Their English was very poor and what was presented to the TV audience as the Czech language was nothing but a mockery of our native tongue.

69

Many of our members arrived here as political refugees. We lost, in many cases, not only all material possessions, but were also separated from our families. Many of us were persecuted by the communist judicial system for our beliefs and many of us spent long terms in communist jails and concentration camps. We came to the United States because we believed in freedom and in the justice and in the future for ourselves and our posterity. Over the years we established ourselves in our new country, served and protected the ideas of the American way of life."

The Czechoslovak Special Interest Group that sent the above, went on to demand an explanation and apology, under threat of a boycott of NBC programming. Our reply pointed out, respectfully and properly, that the Festrunk characters had never been recognized as insulting, but as warmly honest, lovable, appealing human beings, themselves treated with dignity and respect. The humor derived not from ethnicity but from their unfamiliarity with American customs and slang. Thus the satire was directed at the <u>American</u> character; i.e., the male breast fetish, sexual emphasis and the like. The brothers, throughout their *SNL* history, had never demeaned nor insulted their Czechoslovakian heritage, not would we have allowed it. But through the Festrunk brothers, we reflected our own frailties, traits and foibles in a humorous fashion.

So it went, with complaints about stereotyping at various times, in addition to those mentioned, from Jews, Catholics, Protestants, the Elderly, Hispanics, Greeks, Arabs, Italians, Irish, Russian, French, Puerto Ricans, Native Americans, English, Ukrainians, Rumanians, Businessmen, the Disabled, Gypsies and, most unlikely, the Amish, who aren't supposed to watch television! They probably have an attorney, though.

Another reality is perception — even if the project hasn't been produced! A feature picture, *Fort Apache: The Bronx* was a case in point. The story, set in a dangerous Bronx police precinct, starred Paul Newman as a cynical, jaded patrolman, Ed Asner as a tough, unbending captain, and Danny Aiello as a vicious, racist patrolman. Not very positive white role models, to be sure.

NBC had purchased the TV rights for *Fort Apache* from Producer David Susskind before production began and we asked for many script modifications, especially in language. I worked closely with Director Dan Petrie as he shot problematical scenes two ways, thus ensuring a sanitized version for television, excising any objectionable earthiness. We also used caution regarding stereotyping. While it is truthful to say that 90% of the criminals in those neighborhoods are non-white, it is not true that 90% of the non-whites who live there are criminals. Unless we show minorities who are cops, and civilian minorities who are honest citizens, we present a distorted picture that not only hurts law-abiding minorities, but also plays upon the fears of the white majority. The same principle applies to Italian-Americans. Most Mafioso are Italian but most Italians are not Mafioso. Writers on cop shows are very sensitive to that reality.

In spite of our care, and before shooting began, the Bronx community rose in righteous indignation, witness the following excerpts from a love letter to the president of NBC:

> "The Committee Against Fort Apache understands that NBC has purchased the rights to the movie, *Fort Apache; The Bronx.* Since March, the movie has been the target of protests by thousands of Blacks and Puerto Ricans who object to this portrayal as 'violent savages, prostitutes, degenerates, and drug addicts.' In spite of our widely-publicized protests…NBC has decided to buy and eventually air a film that has already been condemned by community groups, politicians, educators, artists, clergy, parents, students, media groups, workers and behavioral scientists…(who) have charged that ' the deleterious effect to the self-image of minority youth and adolescents that will be promoted by the production of

this film is psychologically criminal and goes against the efforts being made by very many individuals and institutions throughout the city to encourage a positive personal and community sense of self-esteem…it is clear that your concern for profits comes before your concern to present positive images of minority communities."

Censorship? What censorship?
—Alfred E. Newman

When you see a fork in the road, take it!
---Luther Conant

I began my so-called career as an NBC Page in 1948, shortly after graduation from college. The Page staff was supposed to be an elite group, chosen for leadership qualities, poise and interpersonal abilities — with the incentive of unlimited opportunity for advancement within the network. Some did move up, but I've always suspected the opportunity pitch was propaganda, enabling NBC to get away with paying us $45 a week! They did, however, provide uniforms, a less-than-thrilling perk for those of us who'd recently returned from World War II military service.

But, my gosh, it was exciting! *Texaco Star Theater* premiered in 1948 and there were still lots of famous radio shows on the air. Sure, we were glorified ushers and messengers, but we did get close to Milton Berle, Perry Como, Fred Allen, *The Voice of Firestone* program, Bishop Fulton J. Sheen, *Howdy Doody, Paul Lavalle and the Cities Service Band of America, The Aldrich Family* and on and on and on.

I still blink when I realize I was associated, even peripherally, with Maestro Arturo Toscanini and the NBC Symphony. Not only did we usher folks in and out of famed Studio 8H, but one might even escort the Maestro to the studio from his car or run messages to his dressing room. I have met literally hundreds of entertainment personalities, yet Toscanini had an aura that I've never experienced since. And popular! Broadcast tickets are complimentary, and the demand for NBC Symphony concerts was incredible. I was frequently assigned to the information booth at the ground floor studio entrance where I was often offered up to $100 for a ticket. Oh, that I had them — me and my $45 a week!

One of the more embarrassing incidents in my life was when I was working in the lobby, "protecting" the studio elevators from riff-raff, especially musicians carrying instruments. They were relegated to a freight elevator that was for the use of tradesmen, carpenters, plumbers and musicians. After all, NBC couldn't have a cello or piccolo contaminate an elevator reserved for NBC executives, their secretaries or the guy from the sandwich shop delivering a BLT to sportscaster Bill Stern. I felt no compunction, therefore, stopping a fiddle player, disdainfully sending him to the freight elevator where he belonged. I guess it makes a good story that the schmuck who was me had just sent Yehudi Menuhin to the freight car! And he went!

The Number One TV Show at that time was *Texaco Star Theater* starring Milton Berle, although none of us realized initially what its impact would be on the television history and business. My particular job was to escort Milton's mother from her car to the studio where she had a reserved seat in the front row. Mrs. Berle has always been considered the quintessential stage mother, but I found her gracious although I was amused by her social metamorphosis as Milton became more and more successful. She was originally Sadie Berlinger, progressing over the years to become Mrs. Sondra Berle.

Production of the Berle show was frantic. After all, 60 minutes of live television each week was a monstrous undertaking and Milton was star, producer, writer, lighting director and resident Hitler. Perhaps there was no other way to do it and Milton was not loved by the production staff, but who's to criticize success? Many people basked in his glory, none more than the NBC Program Executive Warren Wade, a rotund and officious little character who managed a flashy entrance each week, sporting a homburg, trailing a cloud of expensive cigar smoke — and leading a mousy little wife.

One night Milton laid in wait. He'd just experienced his pre-show blow job from his "nurse" (a gorgeous hooker in medical whites, a camouflage that fooled no one) and was feeling mellow, entertaining a crowd of hangers-on in the corridor before the show. Wade made his pompous entrance and greeted Milton with enthusiasm. Milton introduced the Wades to his "nurse." With a sweet "Oh, Mr. Wade, I've heard so much about you!" she proceeded to reach over and grab Wade by the balls. Hard! Well, first the homburg flew to the ceiling, followed by a yipping Warren Wade and his cigar. To no one's surprise, the

75

Wades absented themselves from that show and for the rest of the season.

Even from our lowly positions, we sensed that we were witnessing and were part of something special — something destined to be the greatest influence in the history of communications — for both good and bad. But we didn't know what it was, no one did. Everything was new and fascinating — and crude. These were the days before every junior executive had a computer on his desk and a wall-sized console with television feeds from innumerable channels, and the ability to call up pictures of studio rehearsals, the newsroom, competing stations and cousin Harriet in Dubuque. To view the network, for example, one had to go to a tiny screening room on the sixth floor where the most popular network (the network at that time was New York, Chicago and Philadelphia!) program was fed from Chicago at 5 PM. Top executives, including RCA Chairman, General Sarnoff himself, came to watch *Kukla, Fran and Ollie*! Charming, literate and amusing, it was just a guy with two hand puppets talking with a pleasant, middle-aged lady. And you know what? There are lots of people, including myself, who'd like to see the same simple courtesy and literate conversation return to the tube. Burr Tillstrom and Fran Allison, where are you when we need you?

I left the Page staff in 1949 to try my luck as an actor, then made an abortive stab at organizing a musical theater company in Minneapolis. In the winter! I brought my frozen and unsuccessful bones back east when the ice floes broke up, and got a job as a commercial producer for BBDO. In those early days of television, advertising agencies on behalf of their clients, owned the programs and controlled time periods. I was assigned to the Lucky Strike cigarette account (something I regret to this day) which fully sponsored three prime-time programs — *Your Hit Parade, This is Show Business* and the dramatic anthology *Robert Montgomery Presents*. My responsibility was the commercials — Dorothy Collins peeking out from the Lucky Strike bullseye — and the musical extravaganzas featuring the

Lucky Strike players and singer/spokesman Snooky Lanson. The commercials featured a variety of situations and settings — one week a college classroom, then a beach or restaurant and so forth. The players would deliver little rhymes extolling the many virtues of the product, Snooky would make an impassioned plea to buy at least a carton, then the ensemble would gather around to serenade Lucky Strike with the famous "Be Happy, Go Lucky" song. These epics, produced live, have, perhaps mercifully, not survived, but I saved a couple of whimsical parodies, written in blowsy moments at Hurley's tavern one very late Saturday night. Here's one:

> OPEN ON SNOOKY LEANING AGAINST A DOOR MARKED "LUCKY HOUSE." A BRIGHT RED LIGHT GLOWS ABOVE THE DOOR.

> SNOOKY
> Hi, neighbor. Are you happy with your cigarette and (meaningfully) everything? Well, let's step inside and pay a visit to some ladies of the evening.

> CUT TO INTERIOR. IT IS DIMLY LIT AND ORNATE AND BAROQUE INN STYLE. A STAIRWAY LEADS OFF STAGE RIGHT AND NEAR IT A LITTLE MAN IS MOURNFULLY PLAYING THE PIANO WITH A NERVOUS, QUAVERING HAND. THE BUXOM, CURVACEOUS MADAM IS ON THE STAIRWAY. SEVERAL COUCHES ARE IN THE ROOM AND SEVERAL SCANTILY-CLAD GIRLS RECLINE ON THEM.

> CHORUS
> Be Happy, Go Lucky
> Be Happy, Go Lucky Strike
> Be Happy, Go Lucky
> Go Lucky Strike today!

TWO GIRLS DANCE, UNDULATING THEIR WAY DOWNSTAGE.TWO LUCKY BULLSEYES ARE PLACED STRATEGICALLY ALONG THE UPPER HALF OF THEIR BODIES AND ACROSS THEIR LOINS. IN GLITTER LETTERS IS THE LEGEND "LS/MFT." THE CAMERA DOLLIES IN FOR CU OF GIRL, SMOKING A LUCKY AT END OF LONG CIGARETTE HOLDER.

GIRL (SINGS)

My technique is suited for
An older man or boy
And I can give them just as much
As Luckies' smoking joy!

ON THE LAST LINE SHE GESTURES TOWARD CIGARETTE AND GIVES FORTH A VIOLENT BUMP. THE GLITTER LETTERS TWINKLE GAILY AND PERHAPS PART REVEALINGLY.

CHORUS
Be Happy, Go Lucky
Be Happy, Go Lucky Strike
Be Happy, Go Lucky
Go Lucky Strike Today!

PULL BACK FOR LONG SHOT AS SHE JOINS THE OTHER GIRLS IN THEIR PROVOCATIVE DANCE. THEY SHIMMY THEIR WAY TO THE PIANO AND WRITHE GENTLY, INVITINGLY, EXCITINGLY ABOUT THE PIANO PLAYER. HE LOOKS UP WITH A WAN SMILE.

PIANIST (SINGS)
You've often heard sad stories 'bout

Musicians such as I
But we derive our pleasure from
What's in that red bullseye!

CHORUS
Be happy, Go Lucky
Be Happy, Go Lucky Strike
Be Happy, Go Lucky
Go Lucky Strike Today!

HE CONTINUES TO PLAY WITH RESIGNATION AND THE GIRLS, SPYING THE MADAM, DANCE OVER AND SALAAM TO HER. AS THEY BEND OVER WE SEE WRITTEN ON THEIR HIND PARTS, "BE HAPPY, GO LUCKY."

MADAM (SINGS)
Our prices here are very fair
And pleasure's guaranteed
With Luckies and our ladies
We take care of every need!

AT THIS POINT SHE REACHED INSIDE HER AMPLE BOSOM AND EXTRACTS THREE CARTONS OF LUCKIES AND GIVES ONE TO EACH GIRL. THEY ACCEPT THEM GRATEFULLY AND DANCE OFF MERRILY.

CHORUS
Be Happy, Go Lucky
Be Happy, Go Lucky Strike
Be Happy, Go Lucky
Go Lucky Strike Today!

THE MADAM USHERS IN A MAN WHO CLOSELY RESEMBLES HOMER THROCKHURST,

WHO IS IN TOWN FOR THE NATIONAL CONVENTION OF BUTTER AND EGG MEN. HE HOLDS A LUCKY PACK TO CAMERA.

HOMER (SINGING)
Perfect mildness and rich taste
Are fine in some respects
But I came not for Lucky Strike
I came here for sex!

ON THIS LINE HE THROWS PACK OVER HIS SHOULDER AND THE GIRLS RUSH IN AND BEGIN TO CART HIM UP THE STAIRS. THE MADAM FOLLOWS, CAREFULLY EXTRACTING WALLET FROM HIS POCKET. AS SHE DOES, SNOOKY, LOOKING A BIT WEARY, LETS THEM PASS AND COMES TO FOOT OF STAIRS. THE MADAM HAS GIVEN HIM A SIGN, "WE'RE NOT SO MILD, BUT OH, BROTHER!"

SNOOKY
Neighbor, let me ask you. Are you happy with your present brand of cigarettes...and other things? Well, a recent 438-city survey has shown that millions of people are not. And if you're not, change your Lucky Switch today!

EVERYONE RUSHES BACK DOWN THE STAIRS TO GATHER AROUND SNOOKY FOR FINISH.

ALL
Be Happy, Go Lucky
Be Happy, Go Lucky Strike
Be Happy, Go Lucky
Go Lucky Strike Today!

Man, that's advertising!

The Lucky Strike commercials were well-produced, he says modestly, and won many awards, including the first TV Guide award as commercial of the year, a bronze statuette of an heroic figure holding a filligree globe. We showed it proudly on *Your Hit Parade* one Saturday night and I was appointed its guardian, with orders to return it to the agency safely. The end of the show, however, entailed packing the commercial sets for transport to CBS for use the next evening on *This Is Show Business,* then a pop or two at Hurley's, all the time lugging the trophy. It was not until 1 AM that I taxied back to the office where, in exiting the cab, I hit the statuette against the door and broke off a couple of pieces of the globe. I still cry thinking about that night, scrounging around the art department of an empty ad agency at 2 AM trying to find glue to put poor Atlas and his globe back together. I stayed at the agency for another twenty-five years, so I guess my patch job remained undiscovered.

BBDO was also the agency for the Republican National Committee which meant working on the 1952 presidential campaign, in addition to our regular duties. The hours were killers, but most of us were conservative Republicans, delighted to be part of political and television history.

In retrospect, I've always been mildly ashamed of my involvement with cigarette advertising although it was long before our awareness of the health dangers of smoking. Likewise, I'm more than embarrassed that it was BBDO that was responsible for the 30-second political commercials that inundate us today with "image without substance" advertising, injurious not to our lungs, but to our political health. It was the 1952 campaign that introduced the marketing of a candidate like cereal or soap.

Our candidate, General Eisenhower, contrary to his persona as a kindly old grandfather was, in fact, a crusty (and often vulgar) army general, not kindly disposed to some of the requirements of television. High on that list was the use of makeup, though it was obvious he needed it, as the early harsh lighting of television tended to bounce off his bald dome. BBDO executive Hugh Rogers, an alcoholic genius of early television, was the bearer of the bad news that we'd hired a makeup artist, and the general responded predictably, his language blistering the walls. Bowing to the inevitable, however, he plopped down in the makeup chair, suffering a cloth to be placed around his neck, all the while muttering about the indignity of it all, that makeup was for sissies and fags and fairies and the like. At one point he turned to the very patient, long-suffering makeup man and asked condescendingly, "I suppose you weren't in the army?"

Here's where Hugh Rogers' genius came into play, as the makeup man, a plant, truthfully and simply replied, "101st Airborne, General." The 101st Airborne was Eisenhower's favorite outfit, those paratroopers who had jumped into France, been cut off at Bastogne and where its commanding officer had replied to a German demand to surrender with the historic, "Nuts." As you can imagine, the General shut his mouth and never complained about makeup again.

Not long into the campaign, it became obvious that candidate Eisenhower was a very stiff speaker, so we searched for a more comfortable presentation device rather than formal stump speaking, finally recommending a home library setting wherein he could chat informally with friends, "friends" who were hand-picked, receptive campaign big shots armed with softball questions. Then we needed to find a moderator to introduce the participants, move the questioning along and sum up the discussion. At that time BBDO represented *BF Goodrich Celebrity Time*, sort of panel show hosted by an old-time Hollywood leading man, Conrad Nagel. Nagel was a well-known Republican and he was chosen, at least by us, to host. Nagel, as charming as he could be, was a rather effete character who hadn't made a film in many years, but we couldn't find anyone else, so some poor guy (probably Rogers again) got the job of breaking the news to Eisenhower. "Now, General, we've designed a nice library set, and we think there should be a host and we're recommending...(gulp)...Conrad Nagel." With that, Ike's eyes lit up. "Why, that's wonderful! He's Mamie's favorite actor!" No one dared asked how long it had been since Ike had taken Mamie to the movies.

We also represented the vice-presidential candidate, Richard Nixon, although I met him only once. After producing a radio address in Binghamton, New York, I was allowed to travel back to New York in the campaign plane, a wheezing DC-3 that carried the candidate, his party and the press corps, mostly guys from California who'd covered Nixon for years and had absorbed some of his beliefs. We flew into LaGuardia airport, cruising low along the Hudson River, the lights of New York City shining brightly as we descended. It was one of those perfect views of Manhattan and I suspect that some of the westerners had never seen it like that before. Everyone crowded to one side of the plane for a good view, and I clearly remember one of those hard-bitten reporters looking at the spectacular sight and exclaiming, "We just can't let them take that away!"

I'm not sure he was referring to the Democrats or the Reds!

The Red Scare was in full cry at that time, and the advertising business was a leader in "protecting" its clients from subversion and unpatriotic associations. It wasn't until I was transferred to Hollywood in 1953 that I actually participated in that execrable era in American history, but I've thought about it a lot, rationalizing my personal involvement as a youthful indiscretion, but ashamed, in retrospect, for the sins of the industry. Mark Goodson, the game show maven, wrote an article in the *New York Times* not long ago, describing the shallow, superficial...no, reprehensible procedures we followed to make sure our programs weren't tainted by the inclusion of actors, directors, composers, producers or writers who may have been involved with "subversive" activities.

BBDO's Red Scare guy was Jack Wren, purportedly an ex-FBI agent who "cleared" personnel. From Hollywood we'd teletype cast and production lists to Wren who would reply that so-and-so was "available" or not. (Now there's a code that will stand up in court!) Absolutely no one knew where Jack Wren got his information, nor whether it was accurate, nor did anyone want to know as long as the client was "protected." It's hard to believe that such nonsense was allowed to happen in the United States of America. Shameful.

In 1980, AFTRA, the performer's union, made a presentation to John Henry Faulk, the humorist and bitter victim of the Red Scare tide that had swept the nation in the 50s. The well-deserved tribute to Faulk prompted me to send a letter of catharsis to Bud Wolff, Executive Secretary of AFTRA.

"I was interested to read of the recognition given by your Board to John Henry Faulk. It brought back unpleasant memories for I can think of no single experience over the past thirty years more shameful than involvement, albeit innocent, in the intimidation and 'clearance' process of the 50s. Believe me, I cringed when I saw Woody Allen's *The Front* a few years ago and kept muttering to my wife, 'My God, that's just the way it was!'

Hopefully that experience shall never be repeated. While political blacklisting of actors has been eradicated, dangers still abound and vigilance and education are constantly required. As our mutual pal (and victim) Peter Leeds may have told you, I experienced a situation at BBDO just last year in which I perceived the infringement of the civil rights of an actor denied work because of an unfounded 25 year-old rumor regarding his morals. Perhaps because of the 50s experience I was particularly vocal in my disgust with and criticism of BBDO Management that resulted in pressures precipitating my decision to retire from BBDO.

My argument that work should not be denied because of innuendo, rumor and unsupported gossip was met with the 30 year-old rejoinder about 'protecting the client.' Déjà vu! As it turned out, we fulfilled our contractual commitment to the actor but, surprise, surprise! — the spot never made it out of test. What hurt the most was the realization that I was an anachronism — that the people with whom I was arguing were not there in the 50s. They had no knowledge of, nor had they experienced what we had, and did I feel my age!

The point, of course, is that the 50s experience must be kept alive so that it does not happen again in any form. Therefore AFTRA is to be commended not only for your thanks to Mr. Faulk, but for reminding the broadcast community of this most disgraceful period in our history. Only in that way can today's self-appointed arbiters of morals or whatever be made aware of the equation. I hope it's not too much to ask that our experience of the past shall serve as a lesson for today."

The actor in question was Chuck Connors who, at the time, had been in two or three series including *Roots,* and had established a solid reputation as a western star and right wing citizen of probity and firm belief. He'd appeared on all three networks many times, his background scrupulously checked, yet Chuck had been hounded by a totally unfounded and scurrilous story that he'd been involved with a pornographic gay film in his early days in Hollywood. Considering his public history as a major league ballplayer and his financial comfort before his acting career began, the rumor was patently absurd. Nevertheless, it persisted and came to the attention of an anal BBDO executive who went ballistic when he discovered we were casting Chuck Connors in a commercial. In his zeal to "protect" the client from association with such a pervert, he insisted we terminate the contract. Unfortunately logic, legality, common sense and civil rights are not in the vocabulary of such uptight jerks and no argument moved him from his appointed responsibility. I'm surprised he even let the commercial go to test where, to no one's surprise, it died.

The advertising business in the early 50s was exactly as described in *The Hucksters* — hard-drinking, amoral, pressure-packed — and great fun. 383 Madison Avenue, where BBDO was located, was across 48th Street from the Hotel Roosevelt, and a popular after-hours game was to spy on the hotel rooms in hopes of catching a babe in some form of deshabille with her window shades up. Since we often held meetings in the hotel, we were familiar with the room layout and the room numbers, hence we recognized which room held the action. A famous story, probably apocryphal, was that of the agency president, Charlie Brower, spotting a couple in the throes of intercourse, calling the room, and when the poor guy answered the phone, Charlie, in his most stentorian voice, spoke, "This is God! Aren't you ashamed of yourselves?!"

My favorite, less titillating but true, took place one stifling summer's day before central air conditioning had been installed in the hotel. We spotted a tourist sticking his head out the window, desperately searching for a breath of air. One of our resident jokesters called the guy's room, identifying himself as a hotel security guard, inquiring if the man had been leaning out the window. He explained to the bewildered guest that because New York had so many suicides the hotel had installed an electric beam between the roof and the sidewalk. Thus, when someone leaned too far out the window they broke the beam, alerting security. Would the man please close the window as we wouldn't want an accident, would we? With that the guy closed the window, returned to safety — and a sweltering room with no circulation!

Bruce Barton, one of the founders of BBDO, was semi-retired when I joined the company, but kept an office and came in almost every day although his responsibility was mainly PR, hall-wandering and smooching the prettiest secretaries. (Try that today!) They didn't mind for he was still a handsome and charming old duck, adrip with savoir faire and personality as befits a former congressman, renowned author and founding father. One day a visitor asked Bruce how he spent his day and Bruce replied, " I wake at eight, my valet brings me coffee and the *New York Times*. While sipping coffee I turn to the obituaries and if I'm not listed, I get up and go to the office."

Live television was a constant adventure. When assigned to *Saturday Night Live* in 1979, it was with a real sense of déjà vu, for in the early 50s everything was live. It made for a tough weekend, covering *Your Hit Parade* on Saturday at 10:30 PM, *This is Show Business* at 8 PM on Sunday and *Robert Montgomery Presents* at 9:30 PM every other Monday night (also in 8H!) It was always nervous time when the second hand swept to airtime as you were never sure — of anything. One Christmastime, *Your Hit Parade*, which was telecast from the Center Theater at 49th Street and 6th Avenue, included numbers from the Rockefeller Center skating rink, one of the first remote telecasts. The finale featured Snooky Lanson, Eileen Wilson and the entire cast singing "O, Holy Night," standing under the statue of Prometheus at the rink. This meant that many cast members had only a couple of minutes to get from the theater to the rink, necessitating a run down a flight of steps to the concourse level of Rockefeller Center, a sprint down a long corridor, and exit through a public restaurant to the rink.

Just prior to airtime, I was returning to the theater from the rink when I was horrified to come upon a Rockefeller Center guard blithely locking security gates across the concourse corridor, "What are you doing?! Don't you realize that in about thirty minutes 25 people are going to be tearing ass through here?!!" Of course he didn't know, the carriage of communications had broken another wheel!

Just as one never forgets their first romance, *Your Hit Parade* holds a special place in the hearts of those who worked with it, still recalled almost fifty years later for its inventive technique, good music and pure family entertainment values. Folks still ask about it, especially the top tune survey that was the property of the American Tobacco Company. Rumor had it that the survey was conducted by a professor at Columbia University. All we knew was that producer Dan Lounsbury received a call from an unidentified person on Monday with the survey results and we were off and running, attempting to dramatize "Harbor Lights" for the twentieth straight week, or trying to figure out how the heck to dramatize a Phil Harris classic, "The Thing." It wasn't always easy, but it sure was thrilling to be part of it.

The American Tobacco Company was a major force in the early days of television, full-sponsoring two hours of primetime programming each week. From my perspective *Your Hit Parade* was hard yet exciting work with lousy hours. *Robert Montgomery* was classy and *This is Show Business* was just plain fun. It was broadcast from a Broadway Theater (now David Letterman's) every Sunday. Called a quiz show, in reality it was a variety program in which a panel would chat with artists following their presentation. And what a panel! And what artists! The panel was moderated by Clifton Fadiman and included such luminaries as George S. Kaufman, Abe Burrows, Sam Levenson and Jacqueline Susann, not yet a best-selling author but already the wife of program producer Irving Mansfield. The artists ran the gamut from Metropolitan tenor Richard Tucker to comedian Fat Jack Leonard and stars of the New York City Ballet.

Kaufman was know as an iconoclast and professional curmudgeon with a sardonic wit that got him into deep trouble with the public on at least one occasion. He made a snide remark at Christmas regarding his distaste for "Silent Night," and letters poured in from everywhere, forcing him to make an on-air apology. My acquaintanceship with Kaufman was strictly a nodding one. He nodded when I presented him with a weekly complimentary carton of Luckies, although I once had the unnerving job of actually asking for his autograph! He was well-known for not giving autographs, considering it a common request beneath his dignity. However, an executive at the American Tobacco Company had the bright idea of having all of the American Tobacco on-air personalities sign a special

Christmas card for his young son. What a gracious and thoughtful idea, but not to little old me who had to get the damned card filled out! Apparently they thought I was buddy-buddy with the stars and, admittedly, it was no problem getting the greetings of Snooky Lanson, Eileen Wilson, Dorothy Collins, Clifton Fadiman and even stuffy Robert Montgomery. But I had only that "nodding" acquaintance with George S. Kaufman and, frankly, the man scared the hell out of me. Naturally I saved him for the last (maybe a full card of other autographs would help) and with trepidation I finally approached the great man. He nodded when I gave him his gift carton of Luckies and I popped the question. As I visualized my budding career going bye-bye, he looked at me for a long moment, then nodded (that was twice!), took the pen and signed. Many years later, if he didn't dump it, some undeserving middle-aged man has in his possession what may be the only autograph ever given by George S. Kaufman. I hope he appreciates it.

It is proper to remind ourselves that the American Tobacco Company, Kraft, Philco and others were pioneers, willing to experiment and finance early television, trying all kinds of programs, some good and some not so hot. For every *Your Hit Parade* there was a *Go Lucky* with Jan Murray or *Your Lucky Clue* starring Basil Rathbone. But without those early advertisers and visionaries we would not have free television today. The American Tobacco Company had better luck with another effort, or don't you remember *Meet the Champ?* It was a boxing extravaganza dreamed up by an old time radio personality, Wally Butterworth, best known for his classic radio show, *Vox Pop. Meet the Champ* matched top amateur fighters of the armed forces, duking it out at different military bases around the country. It was amazing how often the matches were held at the Naval Training Center in San Diego. Surely it couldn't have been the weather nor our accommodations at the La Jolla Beach and Tennis Club. Oh, no.

I've always found boxing distasteful, but there I was at ringside each week, splattered with blood and sweat, handing commercial copy to Wally who did the blow-by-blow commentary, badly, as he had no boxing knowledge. To his credit, however, he hired three matchmaker/trainers to work with the boxers, gentlemen who belied everything you've ever heard about the cruelty, dishonesty and criminality associated with boxing. One was former light-heavyweight champion Tommy Loughran, a literate and charming man who worked as a sugar broker at the New York Commodities Exchange. Another was the elderly and sophisticated "Bowtie" Jimmy Bronson, known best as the trainer of heavyweight champion Gene Tunney in the 20s. The other was Billy Cavanagh, once the boxing coach at the United States Military Academy, famous as a great fight referee and arbiter of innumerable title fights in the 20s and 30s. All three personified the approbation of gentle man. It was a privilege to know them.

The most vivid memory of *Meet the Champ* had nothing to do with boxing, but about early, experimental television. One of our shows was from an aircraft carrier moored in San Diego Bay, necessitating a picture transmission across the harbor to a series of relay stations, terminating in Los Angeles which would then feed the embryonic ABC television network. The first relay station was a place called Red Mountain and the technical rehearsal at 5 PM worked perfectly. The show, however, was at 7 PM and we discovered to our horror that sunset, for whatever reason, affected the picture. Remember, this was 1952 and remote broadcasting was in its infancy. I can still hear director Charlie Russhon screaming, "Find Red Mountain! Find Red Mountain!" as the picture needle kept sliding to zero and we were off the air. I hope ABC had a standby film ready, for we didn't make the schedule that evening.

I was not personally involved with the commercial scandals—marbles in the soup, open windows purporting to be clear glass — but I was a witness to a couple of more innocent bits of chicanery, both for that popular automobile, DeSoto. My first out-of-town trip was to Detroit for a production meeting discussing the debut of the 1952 model line. The president of

90

DeSoto was an engineer named Keller and the agency tried to dazzle him with some progressive commercials showing the car actually in motion — running shots, open highway, acceleration — the works. Mr. Keller took one look at the storyboards and asked but one question, "Where are the flowers and the turntable?" It seems that new cars were historically introduced at the Detroit Auto Show on turntables surrounded by banks of flowers. Back to the drawing board. Of course everyone can recall the revised introduction of the 1952 DeSoto. Its turntable really stood out from that of Buick, Ford and Chevrolet.

Our mild chicanery was to load the trunk of the car with weights to make the car appear rakish and to polish it with milk which made it shine a bit better on television. I wonder if Mr. Keller noticed. I guess it worked, for it took another decade before DeSoto went out of business and by that time they'd joined the rest of the industry in actually demonstrating the car on the road, something it was, after all, built to do.

Television brings into your home people
You wouldn't have in your own home.
— **Fred Allen**

NBC occasionally purchased feature pictures from Hollywood studios and I was delegated to review and edit these films for television. Often we were able to use the well-sanitized airline versions, yet there were times that the editing process was time-consuming and difficult. You haven't lived until you've seen *Protocol* a dozen times, I'm a fan of Goldie Hawn, but...

I can remember several pictures vividly. First on my "ughhh!" list is a piece of dreck, *Elvira, Mistress of the Dark*. For the uninitiated, Elvira was a fully-developed witch-like creature with stringy hair and boobs hanging to the ground, but with an innocent heart of gold that got her into situations not of her own doing. It seems that Brandon Tartikoff, president of the network, wished to develop a feature picture division, unwisely choosing Elvira and her personality as his first three stars. The picture was so filled with cheap sex jokes and innuendo that I pronounced it unacceptable. The boss' reply — "Bill, this is a Tartikoff production. It would be highly embarrassing to all of us if this film did not appear on NBC. It doesn't make any difference what you do. Make it acceptable."

Well, that message was pretty simple, so I tried, much to my regret. It was awful.

Editing notes follow:

ELVIRA, MISTRESS OF THE DARK

1:20	Make sure KSFB are fictional call letters
1:40	"...the gal with the enormous (looks at breasts)...ratings
2:15	"...the Head with two things..."
2:25	"...the gal who put boobs back into the boob tube."
3:25	"...the ladies back home call me Longhorn. Maybe you can guess why."
3:35	"...the sooner I get in the saddle the better..."

3:45   "…it's just gonna be you and your trusty right hand."

3:55   "…I need this job like a leper needs a 3-way mirror."

4:00   "…Milkin' time!" (and action as Earl grabs Elvira's breasts)

4:15   "…I'll tie your weenie in a granny knot."

4:25   "…you said she was a nympho!"

4:30   "…crapola"

7:25   (here, and in other places, delete all shots of personalized license plate, "KICKASS.")

9:00   (Delete shot and SFX as man flatulates)

9:50   (Delete shot of man crudely picking nose)

9:50   (Delete shot from inside car of Elvira with breasts flattened against windshield)

10:20   (Delete shot of man picking rear end)

10:50   (Delete closeup of bosom as Elvira drops hot dog into cleavage)

12:20   "…I'll beat it out of you." (Action with breasts)

13:10   "…what I wouldn't do for one peek at those gazongas."

13:45   "…nice tits."

16:45   "…How about a virgin?"… "Maybe. But I'll have a couple of drinks first."

17:00   (This scene, in the bar of the bowling alley, is unacceptable as produced. Certainly considerable dubbing/editing will be necessary. Hopefully alternate footage is available.)

18:40   "…careful, you could put somebody's eyes out with those." (Reference to Patty's breasts)

20:20   "…I'd rather squeeze into my (provocative look) — agenda."

24:15   "…I need a house like I need a padded bra."

25:00   "…you really got shafted."

25:15   (Delete Chastity's take as Elvira tells Vincent, "I'll do it for fifty bucks.")

26:35 "...passing out condoms to kindergardeners."
28:05 "...does a chicken have a pecker?"
30:00 "...don't get your panties in a bunch."
30:30 "...good thing I'm leaving, the neighbors would never get any sleep." (Reference to noisy bed springs)
31:00 (Entire undressing scene must be re-cut to lose provocative costuming and gratuitous, sensual action.)
32:45 "...Did you see those gazongas?"
34:55 (Delete first shot of Elvira's rump thrust into camera)
35:00 "...just grab your tool and start banging."
37:40 "...a cheap whore!"
38:30 (Delete shot of Glotter looking at her breasts)
38:50 (Delete shot of Glotter approaching her from rear as she bends over)
39:05 (Trim as Glotter approaches her, losing business of throwing her over couch)
40:10 "...heck, I was six inches from selling this house today."
41:10 (Lose all business and dialogue as Billy eats edible panties)
42:45 "...How's your head?... "Haven't had any complaints yet"... "Excuse me?"
43:10 "...ooh, I thought that cleared up."
43:20 "...and I'm flat busted...I mean I'm broke."
43:45 (Cut from Elvira mounting ladder to shot of Chastity, back to Elvira falling, losing all marquee business about word "fuck")
47:45 "...tell them I was more than just a great pair of boobs."
47:55 "...I never turned down a stranger for that matter."
49:55 (Delete shot of kid with hole in rear of pants)
50:55 "...guaranteed standing ovulation."

53:00 (Lose tight closeup of rear end in dance number)

54:20 "…bench-sniffing real estate letch, who wants his commission in the sack."

54:00 "…here's to my big opening" (reaction shot)… "I mean…oh, forget it" (leering look at Bob's derriere)

58:10 "…it looks like caca doodoo"

59:10 (Recut and shorten scene as "gremlin" arises from casserole, diminishing sound effects and losing closeups and splattering of guts when the gremlin is shoved into disposal)

63:40 "…such a spaz attack"

67:30 (Sequence wherein townspeople lose their inhibitions must be re-cut. Hopefully there is alternate footage. "Hot dog" and "taco" dialogue and action unacceptable. Chastity straddling man's face and men and women in underwear unacceptable.)

71:00 (Scene in town council chambers to be edited and/or dubbed. Sexual dialogue not acceptable)

71:55 "…she might enjoy that too much."

73:00 "…if I had a broom, I know exactly where I'd put it."

75:10 "…I musta done too much antacid in the 60s"

75:50 (Delete business of priest fondling Elvira's breasts)

77:00 (Lose priest shaking holy water in procession to funeral pyre)

84:30 (lose closeup as Elvira breaks chains with her breasts)

84:55 (Trim, losing Travis touching Elvira's breasts)

85:10 (Re-cut scene in house as Vincent confronts Elvira. Delete closeup of hand being severed and business with it crawling around floor)

91:00 (Re-cut final number in Las Vegas, specifically losing tassel-twirling demonstration)

96:05   END

Makes you want to rush over to Blockbuster for the video,
doesn't it?

Sometimes purportedly intelligent critics and columnists
made life difficult. The following diatribe (edited) was written
by the normally incisive television critic Gary Deeb who must
have been viewing a different picture from me, as evidenced by
the editing notes which follow his column:

> "...it now develops that NBC has purchased network
> TV rights to the Brian De Palma thriller *Dressed to Kill*
> — and the peacock network bluenoses already are
> sharpening their hatchets. The stylish murder mystery
> stars Angie Dickinson and Michael Caine. Rated "R,"
> it's graphically sexy and frighteningly violent. One of
> the most memorable moments in *Dressed to Kill* is the
> elevator murder scene in which Dickinson gets hacked to
> death by a razor-wielding nut, a sequence for which De
> Palma obviously was inspired by the legendary shower
> slaying in Alfred Hitchcock's *Psycho*.
>
> But *Dressed to Kill* still ranks as an intriguing,
> disturbing and mentally stimulating movie. As long as
> viewers are warned enough in advance — so that
> relatively few people stumble into it by accident —
> there's no reason why it shouldn't play on TV with little
> or no editing.
>
> The NBC ax job on *Dressed to Kill* will be carried
> out despite the fact that the movie already has been
> telecast in uncut form on many pay-TV and pay-cable
> systems across the country.
>
> It's understood that NBC ponied up $6.5 million for
> three telecasts of *Dressed to Kill*...but if the same nasty
> fate that wrecked (*Animal House)* also savages *Dressed
> to Kill*, then NBC will be providing yet another

97

commercial for pay-TV, which keeps stealing viewers away from the major networks and local stations.

Because the more NBC, CBS and ABC insist on using popular movies as come-ons — and then actually televise severely watered-down versions of these blockbusters — the more the audience will react with anger and desert 'regular television' in favor of the premium pay-channels, where viewers at least are treated like they possess a modicum of discernment."

Gee, Gary, I'm sorry, but I don't believe that Angie Dickinson giving a guy a blow job in the back of a taxi, nor watching her throat being slit in gruesome detail is really appropriate for living room family enjoyment. Here are my editing notes.

DRESSED TO KILL

2:15 (Dickinson nude in shower, erotically stimulating herself. Bare breasts and pubis shown)

4:15 (Dickinson and husband copulating)

7:30 "Are you working on your peter?"

10:30 (Dickinson-Caine session)— "He gave me a wham-bang special," "I moaned with pleasure at his touch"

11:15 "Tell him he stinks in bed?"

11:45 "Would you sleep with me?"

13:15 (Hand on girl's rear in museum)

15:15 (Nude painting shown in this and subsequent scenes in museum)

22:00 (Graphic sex play in rear seat of cab)

24:50 (Nudity as she puts on bra)

28:00 (Flashback panties dropping)

30:00 (Viewing of letter referring to venereal disease)

33:45   (Killing in elevator...slash on hand, razor slashing, hand sticking from elevator)

37:40   "Blonde bitch!" (VO)

43:00   " When intercourse? What the fuck is it to you?"

44:00   "Hot pants broads...down on her in cab...for Christ's sake...blow by blow description."

44:14   (Discussion of sexual problems)

47:45   "Everybody's getting laid...I didn't say I was getting laid."

48:00   "Lets cut this shit."

48:30   "You're a whore."   (3)... "and who are you fuckin'...fuck you...no, fuck you."

49:45   "that's bullshit!"

49:10   "So who were you fuckin'?"

49:55   "Your ass..."

55:25   "That nosy bitch."

56:00   "hell of a way to lose a patient...should fuck them...cockteaser."

57:00   "Do you think this guy'll go for $500?"

57:40   "Thank God straight fucks are still in style."

64:15   "This bitch is botherin' me...fuckin' ass we can fuck it."

64:45   "Where the fuck were you?" (We have concerns in this scene, on the subway platform, not only about the language but about stereotyping of the punks and the black officer. This scene can be shortened.)

71:45   "Wise ass remarks"

76:15   "Just my ass...my ass"

78:30   (Graphic description of Allen's fantasy)— "he drops his pants...forces me to knees etc")

79:40   (Sex discussion)

80:45   "Do you want to fuck me? I've fucked doctors. Fucked a lot of them, too"

81:45   (Allen costuming; garter belt, etc)..."bulge in your pants."

82:00   "I think you're full of shit."
83:00   "Back to the mind-fuck"
88:45   "Got turned on...Elliot's penis became erect."
90:30   "Grow breasts...don't get hard."
91:00   "Penectomy...take your penis and slice it...castration, reconstruction etc....artificial vagina..."
94:30   (Killing in Bellevue, zipping uniform of nurse.)
96:00   (Nude Allen in window)
96:30   (Nude Allen in shower)
101:00 (Slash across neck)

In fairness, what critic Deeb may have been espousing, was exactly what I thought as I watched the film for the fifth or sixth time in Brian De Palma's editing room — why the hell did NBC buy the picture in the first place!

But under the circumstances, I was proud of the job performed on a very difficult project — retaining the integrity of the plot, horror and characterizations — without much of the gore and graphic sexual activity. That, of course, is the challenge of television editing — to keep the sense and entertainment value even while excising that material which the majority of the audience would find unacceptable in their living rooms — not easy in these days of intellectual and scatalogical freedom in the motion picture industry.

In 1992, Al Schneider, retired vice president of policy and standards for ABC-TV, wrote a letter to the *New York Times* at the time that Time-Warner was being criticized for marketing controversial material and artists, primarily in the recording business. His remarks, in my view, neatly defined corporate responsibility in the entertainment field. They are as prescient today as they were ten years ago:

"The article about Time Warner's standards for product acceptability conjures up the debate I engaged in for 30 years pursuing program guidelines for the ABC

Television Network. The task of defining corporate responsibility in terms of integrity, decency, taste and enlightenment is in constant conflict with the forces of free-marketplace competition and profit motivation.

In the 1970s and the early 80s, with only three networks and no cable, VCRs or satellite distribution channel to cope with, defining corporate policy was less complex. A balance could more readily be struck between containing offensive, tasteless material, presenting taboo-breaking dramatic fare and achieving audience and financial success. Diversity of offerings was a key, and the threat of competitive advantage, while real, was tempered by the ever-present regulatory admonition: a call 'to the Hill' (Congress) to account for program excesses or sensationalism.

Today, with a proliferation of distribution systems, all with vociferous appetites, little room is left for thoughts of appropriateness of material for all the people all the time. This is an era of money-driven morality, in which innovation, shock and gratuitous exploitation override considerations of balance, quality, image, taste and social responsibility.

Success breeds courage, and leadership demands it. When integrity and image once again command respect, and knowledge and information are no longer disparaged as elitist, standards will emerge to guide inventiveness. Not only must the product supplier mirror society, it must lead as well. Cutting edge is acceptable when reason and perspective are its handmaiden.

What it really is all about is *caring* — caring that we balance freedom of expression with truth and accuracy; caring that we expose unbridled sexuality with understanding and commitment in personal relationships; caring that the energy for peaceful harmony quells racial bigotry and that training and education curtail police brutality. Corporate responsibility in setting standards is no more or less than establishing criteria for caring in a competitive free-enterprise system that places excellence and enrichment over debauchery and self-indulgence."

Right on, Al.

Motion pictures, as we know, have become more and more raunchy, so it was no shock that my sewer-mouthed friend, Eddie Murphy, opted for Hollywood's freedom, rather than accede to the restrictions we placed on his love of the vulgar. I fail to understand why the word "fuck" is considered a surefire source of laughs, but Eddie and other contemporary comics seem to think so. My personal view is contained in a satirical note I sent to Eddie's writers, ex-SNL scribes (and friends) Barry Blaustein and David Sheffield, after screening Eddie's feature, *Coming to America.*

"I recently saw *Coming to America*, subtitled 'Solomon and Pudge get a Haircut' and enjoyed it very much. I thought the plot was somewhat predictable, but the performances and production values were first-rate and the dialogue crackled with wit and sophistication. The obligatory cock joke ('The royal penis has been washed') was hilarious and each 'fuck you!', 'up your ass!' and 'no shit!' evoked gales of laughter.

With each incisive gibe I was reminded of the great satirists in literary history—Moliere, Addison and Steele, Swift, Daniel Defoe and others — whose efforts were diluted and restricted by the social mores of their time. Just think, wouldn't it have been dramatically powerful for Friday to turn to Robinson Crusoe and say, 'Up your honky ass, motherfucker!'

Ah, well, we can only thank God that we live and create in an enlightened age when such insightful and

102

intellectually stimulating writing is encouraged and accepted.

Hope your family is well. Love to you and to Eddie who, in a word, was great!"

Before we're too harsh on the motion picture business, however, let's save a little ammunition for television. Howard Stringer, CBS Broadcast Group president, said in 1990, "Producers who work with us will be given open throttle...we could not have put *Married, with Children* on the air when it first started. Now we could. That corner is being pushed...more children watch it than any show on CBS." He added that snaring young viewers was the name of the game with advertisers. One of his producers added, "The shows that have an edge and a point of view and an attitude and who are not...smacky-faced TV kids...I think are going to be appealing. I've got some bad news for you if you don't think that those kinds of words are said and that kids in those age groups are saying them. We're just trying to do a real show here."

Mr. Stringer, Mr. Producer and Gary Deeb, please lock yourselves in a room somewhere and shout "shit" and "fuck" at each other. And take your teenage children with you.

103

Sure, I believe in censorship.
After all, I made a fortune out of it!

— Mae West

The biggest complaint about *Saturday Night Live* over the years was that it was "tasteless." Well, just what is "taste?" What may be tasteless to one is inoffensive to another. How can one group feel revulsion at the death penalty while another senses only proper justice? How can a teenager reject a classical symphony yet extract pleasure listening to three amplified chords from a rock band? What makes Paul Newman pour time and money into auto racing while Jack Nicklaus "wouldn't cross the street to watch the Indy 500?" Why is my taste right and yours so confused?

Taste resists analysis, although many have tried.

Dr. Richard Gilbert — "Taste is the sense of the appropriate."

Dr. Theodore Gill — "Taste is a personal assessment of the quality, the 'rightness' and the fitness of a piece...good taste is especially the taste of cultivated observers"

Webster — "Individual preference; inclination; critical judgement, discernment, or appreciation; manner or aesthetic quality indicative of such discernment or appreciation."

Shakespeare — "Things sweet to taste prove in digestion sour."

It's a fine line that Shakespeare, in his infinite wisdom, describes. In the Jean Doumanian era of *Saturday Night Live*, there was a deliberate attempt to be tasteless. Her philosophy was there should be one raunchy, shocking or vulgar piece in each show. Thus we were subjected to "Peenie Pads," the male sanitary napkin, "Macho Wipes," a sandpapered toilet tissue for strong men, or this delightful laugh-a-thon she actually presented as a candidate for production:

NEWSCASTER (CHARLIE)

We have with us tonight Dr. Calvin Zucco who caused quite a controversy with his theory of the myth of the female orgasm. Dr. Zucco.

GILLIE (IN WHITE COAT)

That's right, Charlie, there's no such thing as the female orgasm. Women don't have orgasms. It's all gonna be in my new book, "Foreplay or Just Plain Stalling." I mean I've gone to bed with a lot of women, and not one of them has had an orgasm. Doesn't that tell you something? I know what you're gonna say — what about the clitoris, right? Well, I've done a lot of research. The clitoris was invented in the late 60s. Not every woman has a clitoris. Jane Fonda has a clitoris. Helen Reddy, maybe. Debbie Reynolds doesn't have one. So don't go throwing clitorises at me and next time a woman says to you don't stop yet, I haven't achieved an orgasm, you say, sorry, coach, no more pushups tonight.

CHARLIE

Thank you, Doctor Zucco

***

It's mind-boggling, isn't it, that supposedly intelligent and insightful writers, performers and producers would actually present such a piece of garbage for consideration on a television network. Now, that one was easy to reject. Just a simple, "For God's sake, are you serious?!"

Yet, and here we go again, I was overruled on the acceptance of the following. Apparently the company was not ready for farting on television. It was funny, though.

OPEN ON MODEL OF COLLEGE FRAT HOUSE

DISSOLVE TO GARY, BRAD AND EDDIE IN
DORM ROOM

BRAD

Hey, guys, listen to this! (CUPS HANDS, MAKES
NOISE)

GARY

Look at this. A double whoopee. (GARY,
SHIRTLESS, CUPS HANDS UNDER ARMPITS AND
MAKES NOISES.BRAD LIGHTS CIGARETTE)

EDDIE

Gimme your matches, man. (EDDIE LIGHTS A
MATCH, BENDS OVER, HOLDING MATCH
BEHIND HIM)

Watch this, guys, you're not going to believe it.

CUT TO: JOE, AS SMOKEY THE BEAR

JOE

There's nothing funny about setting fire to
flatulence. Each year thousands of youngsters take a
chance and lose. What about you? (HOLDS UP PAIR
OF JEANS WITH REAR END BURNED OUT.
SMOKE CURLS FROM BURNED EDGES)

Do you want to become a statistic?

DISSOLVE TO MODEL OF HOUSE, WE HEAR
VOICES

VOICES

God, that was great! That flame must've been two
feet long! Let me try it!

SFX MATCH BEING STRUCK. THE MODEL
EXPLODES, BLOWING ROOF OFF HOUSE. LITTLE

William G. Clotworthy

DOLLS FLY OUT. CHROMAKEY JOE OVER SMOLDERING MODEL

JOE
Don't be foolish. Don't fart around with fire.

(Author's note: In September, 2000, I caught a sitcom in which a scene was set in an elementary school. Parents had been called in to witness a mock trial run by the children. The judge was a stern little girl of ten who, at one point, turned to a little boy about to act up, saying, " Stop it, Brian, there will be no arm farts.")

Returning to Dr. Theodore Gill's definition of taste, the Broadcast Standards editor must, indeed, be a cultivated observer for he is, in fact, imprinting his taste upon others. But, if we can't define taste, how can we justify some schlepper telling you what's tasteful, and what isn't? First of all, think back upon making television acceptable to the majority of a large and culturally diverse national audience. Then think of a trained observer studying the material and making a value judgement on your behalf. You may not totally agree, but majority rules!

Taste in art is like taste in food. For centuries people have compared the judgement of the taste buds with the judgement of the arts. Both are subjective, hence private, thus causing them to be compared. But the philosopher Immanuel Kant suggests that it would be better if our responses to a play (television?) were based on sight or hearing or touch, for that way you'd know that the other saw or heard or felt the same thing. When you taste food or sip wine you can't be confident that the taste buds of your dinner partner will agree with yours.

Parents who attempt to instill in their children an appreciation of good food and dietary habits know the problem. McDonald's cardboard burgers and goose-greased french fries inevitably get the thumbs up while the broccoli and spinach get the "yuk." So the helpless parents learn to defer to these juvenile judgements, biding their time in hopes that taste will be cultivated by degrees, time and knowledge.

But don't count on it!

The same response occurs in the arts. One looks at *Saturday Night Live* or *Jerry Springer* or *Drew Carey* and decides if it is good, bad or indifferent. It doesn't do any good to push *Hamlet* on someone who prefers *Star Trek,* or the ballet on someone who's crazy about Madonna. That person doesn't care whether something is "good for you," or that Roger Ebert recommended it — he just knows what he likes.

Dr. Gill, the noted author and ethicist, also noted that nature endows us with a variety of tastes, both good and bad. Some folks can see or hear better, others have superior senses of touch. And, with proper cultivation, some people are better judges of food or art (or even television) than others. *The New York Times* would not entrust art reviewing to a color-blind critic, nor music criticism to a tone-deaf person. We wonder, however, if the *Times* uses such standards in employing its television critics?

One need not be tone-deaf, color-blind nor a television critic, however, to be the hanging judge of this Eddie Murphy epic:

OPEN ON BAR. THREE GUYS ENTER. THEY ARE VERY UNHIP BUT DON'T REALIZE IT. THEY ARE IN FLORIDA AT A GREY PANTHERS SINGLES BAR, EVERY CUSTOMER IS AT LEAST 85, THE GUYS ARE IN THEIR 20S.

EDDIE
Are you guys sure we can score in this joint?

JOE
Look, these girls are real easy. I've scored every time I've come in here.

MICHAEL
Same with me.

EDDIE

Yeah, but these chicks are kind of old, guys.

MICHAEL

You ever been to bed with an 85 year-old woman? They're sex machines!

JOE

They're monsters. They'll rip you apart. (100 YEAR-OLD WOMAN PASSES BY) Don't even look at her. She's wild, you couldn't handle her.

MICHAEL

Yeah, one night she took on the both of us and I thought we were gonna die.

***

Well, there was another few minutes of the same, including a description of Eddie's eventual partner — "her breasts are so long I swear she has to tuck them into her pants." That sketch received neither the Good Housekeeping Seal of Approval, the AARP Medal of Excellence — nor my okay!

That sketch, of course, was well beyond the pale, not that *Saturday Night Live* was not often "naughty," as identified with such gems as Tim Kazurinsky's "Doctor Jack" who described various ailments with groaning puns, i.e., "Tennis players have Bjorn Borgasms." My two favorites "naughties," were "Doctor Shockley's House of Sperm," and a beautifully constructed skit called "The Party." In the latter, the scene was an elegant 18th-century drawing room where the guests, dolled up in periwigs, knee britches, decollete gowns, etc are introduced by footman Garrett — The Duke of Argyle (in plaid), Lord and Lady Wilkinson (with crossed swords), The Earl of Sandwich (being served meat inside pieces of bread), all preceding Lord and Lady

Douchebag whose entrance led to a series of remarks such as "There's always been a Douchebag in Parliament!" and "Spoken like a true Douchebag!" Lady Douchebag asks for vinegar and water dressing on her salad, etc. Cerebral? Of course not, but it was funny. Some folks criticized the sketch, but since we advertise feminine hygiene products in the *Seven o'clock News*, I didn't see any problem with running it at 11:30 Saturday night. Certainly, I think the sketch was no less tasteless than the adult diaper, anti-diarrhea and laxative commercials telecast at dinner time!

The other sketch I loved was "Doctor Shockley's House of Sperm," telecast at the time when a certain Nobel Prize winner was selling his sperm in some sort of disgraceful attempt to improve the species. *SNL*'s view involved a retail sperm store at which every customer asked for the sperm of Host Rodney Dangerfield. Rodney was in the back room trying to satisfy the clientele with the aid of *Playboy*, then poking his face out from the curtains every few minutes to beg off. It was college humor in its lowest form. Authors Doug Hill and Jeff Weingrad called it undistinguished, but I thought it was hilarious.

A writer once asked me what was the first thing I did when I read a script and I said, " I laugh." After all, I'm human and enjoy a good giggle, no matter how scatalogical, stereotypical, offensive — or unacceptable. After I laugh, then I go to work with the scissors, blue pencil, screaming or begging.

I dislike censorship. Like an appendix it is useless when inert
and dangerous when active.
— **Maurice Edelman**, 1966

Of all the people I dealt with on *SNL*, Al Franken was definitely the most formidable censor fighter. Al is smart, aggressive and relentless, a deadly combination. He's also, I think, a good friend and I know he's a good family man. I respect Al for his intelligence and his sense of humor, although it wasn't always in sync with mine. "The Franken Decade" was an inspired bit of social satire and I enjoyed his book, *Why Not Me?* about the Franken presidential campaign and administration even though he failed to name me to head the National Endowment of the Arts, surely an oversight.

One of my longest battles with Al involved a sketch he wrote called "What's My Addiction?" patterned after the old game show, *What's My Line?* Instead of guessing occupations, however, the panelists had to guess the drugs to which the guests were addicted.

At the time, we'd become much more restrictive as regards drug and alcohol humor. The permissiveness of the seventies was no longer acceptable as the networks, and everyone else, recognized drugs and alcohol abuse as one of the nation's most serious problems. Drugs just weren't funny.

Therefore my first reaction to the sketch was that it poked fun at addiction and recovery programs. We don't pretend to be experts on everything, however, so we did something unusual, we submitted the sketch to an outsider, Doctor Lloyd Johnston of the University of Wisconsin, a leading expert on addiction, who confirmed our feeling that the sketch ridiculed serious addiction problems. It was rejected.

Well, Al was very upset. He knew people with problems and his intention was to show how widespread addiction was, and the inter-relationship between different addictions. He was convinced that the material was anti-drug, so never-say-die Al wrote to Doctor Johnston... "the underlying intent is to show that chemical dependency is destructive, and that whether the substance is alcohol, prescription, or street drugs, it's all basically the same disease. As you may know, this is the position of the drug rehabilitation community, which provides the same treatment for alcoholics, drug addicts and cross-addicted dependents." He followed up with a phone call to Doctor Johnston and before we knew it the good doctor had reversed himself and now agreed with Al! Hoisted on our own petard, we approved the sketch. Here's the idea:

OPEN ON TITLE GRAPHIC: WHAT'S MY ADDICTION?

PARDO (VO)
It's What's My Addiction? And here's our host...former First Lady and recovering alcoholic and valium addict, Betty Ford!

CUT TO GAME SHOW SET. JAN AT DESK.
Thank you, Don Pardo and welcome to "What's My Addiction? — the show where chemical dependency is put right out in the open where it ought to be. So, let's go right ahead and meet our celebrity panelists...Johnny Cash.

CUT TO PHIL AS JOHNNY CASH

Liza Minelli

CUT TO NORA AS LIZA MINELLI
And David Crosby

CUT TO JON AS DAVID CROSBY
Johnny, welcome back.

PHIL
Thank you, Betty.

JAN

You know, we've had a lot of celebrity panelists on our show, but I don't think any of them plays the game as well as you.

PHIL

Well, Betty, I've seen it all and I've done it all. In a way maybe the living hell that I went through drinkin' and druggin' all those years was just the Higher Power's way of auditioning me for this show.

JAN

Well, thank you, Johnny. Now, Liza, I don't think we've had a panelist who has as much fun on the show as you do.

NORA

What can I say? It's a lot more fun guessing someone else's addiction than figuring out my own. (Laughs.)

JAN

And David Crosby. I'd like to welcome you to the show. It's your first time, and I'm sure you'll catch on.

JON

Man, I'm not saying I haven't had my problems, I just want to write some songs, man, and get on with my life.

JAN

Good luck. Well, panelists, let's meet our first addict. She's a housewife from Yorba Linda, California. Please welcome Patricia McManus. (VICTORIA ENTERS AND SITS NEXT TO JAN.) Panelists, Patricia has been addicted for seven years to a drug that

115

can be easily obtained at most suburban shopping malls. We'll start the questioning with Johnny Cash.

***

The panel did not determine Patricia's addiction which turned out to be lithium, but had no trouble with guest Steve Stein, an investment broker who "had been addicted for only eighteen months, but in that time he has lost his Scarsdale home, two BMWs and a thirty foot sailboat." Apparently the investment broker occupation was too obvious a hint and panelist Cash correctly guessed cocaine.

Then the panelists were blindfolded for the introduction of mystery guest Boy George (Bandleader Paul Shaffer) before gathering together at the close to deliver the Alcoholics Anonymous creed.

After the show, we got so many complaints from health-care professionals that we reversed ourselves again and deleted the sketch from the re-run schedule. And we didn't call on Doctor Johnston for expert advice again, either.

Of course what Al and I were discussing was <u>perception</u>. Al's motives and intentions were honest, but our function was to understand what the viewer's perception would be and the broadcast proved that the sketch trivialized addiction and was contrary to our drug policy.

Drug humor was probably the issue that bollixed those of us in Standards more than any other. Our Standards and Practices handbook stated emphatically that "the use of illegal drugs or the abuse of legal drugs shall not be encouraged or shown as socially acceptable." Unfortunately, by the time I came in, that policy had been violated for years by *Saturday Night Live.* Anyone who watched the show consistently couldn't help but get the clear impression that virtually the entire cast, especially John Belushi, used and abused both legal and illegal drugs constantly. That such material got on the air at all demonstrates a nasty little truth about network television — when a show is making lots of money, the boundaries of permissibility get stretched to accommodate it.

Toward the end of my tenure, NBC's policy regarding drug humor tightened up considerably. I'd like to say that we in Standards in New York reasserted ourselves out of renewed moral commitment to fight the scourge of drug abuse in our country, but in truth it happened almost by accident. Bob Hope, of all people, submitted a monologue in 1982 for one of his Specials that contained several jokes about athletes and politicians using drugs, i.e., "...selling coke today, you can get twenty years in prison or two years in Congress."

An editor in the Standards Department on the West Coast suggested to Hope that the drug stuff be minimized. Hope not only agreed, he gave an interview to *Hollywood Variety* in which he stated, approvingly, that NBC had a new policy — no drug jokes whatsoever. This was the first we'd heard of it, but since Bob Hope said in the interview that he'd discussed the matter with NBC Chairman Grant Tinker, we felt it judicious to go along, happily I might add. Hence a new, or reconstituted, Standards policy was born. It remains in effect to this day (or does it?), probably to the chagrin of the writers on *Saturday Night Live*, although they kept on trying. Drugs are amusing again, or haven't you watched FOX lately?

Remember Bartles and James, the dopey farmers who peddled wine coolers? Brilliant satirist A. Whitney Brown submitted a spoof:

"Ed and I want to talk to you about a very important subject—crack. Many of your beatniks and hooligans are being led astray by the new drug craze. But it is not hep to blow crack. For one thing it is a very stupid name. Now Ed and I tried just about everything when we were young. But fortunately we were able to stop before suffering permanent damage. Right, Ed? (ED NODS) So don't be a fool. Why do you think they call it dope? When you want to catch a buzz, pick yourself up three or

117

four cases of our delicious wine coolers. Don't let crack
put you off track. And thank you for your support."

On one hand, that is a smart piece, using the famous
characters in a satirical swipe at the hypocrisy of using
advertising as an anti-drug forum while at the same time
advertising addictive alcohol beverages. The line "we were able
to stop before suffering permanent damage" is particularly
telling. Alas, the parody was interpreted as using drugs for
humor and consequently rejected.

But sometimes things don't go away and A. Whitney Brown,
perhaps taking a page from the Al Franken book, wasn't about to
give up his sketch and worked with us cooperatively as follows:

"Ed and I have just read about a serious new
problem we would like to bring to your attention. Crack.
Now when we first heard about crack, we thought it was
something else. But it is not. Crack is a drug. It is also a
poison. Now Ed and I tried a lot of fool things when we
were young. But fortunately we stopped before we
suffered any permanent damage, eh, Ed? Why, one time
Ed put a penny on a railroad track and it got real big.
Right, Ed? (ED NODS AND GESTURES HOW BIG)
But crack is a different matter. Even a little bit can cause
you to become very stupid. That is what makes people
do it a second time. Crack is a killer drug. Take it from
us, it is nice to grow old. You can sit on the porch and
stare at things all day. Or you can wave at people as they
drive by. These things are very hard to do if you are
dead. If you want to have a good time, pick up a pack or
two of our delicious wine coolers. And thank you for
your support."

That approach was considered anti-drug and was approved.
Drugs were part of the problem I had with Sam Kinison, the
worst scumbag I ever had to deal with on SNL. Sam was a

former street preacher whose schtick was to appear in a long black coat, wearing a beret and shouting jokes at the top of his voice. Our first set-to occurred the night of October 18, 1986, when he was a guest comedian on the show. He ran through his monologue for me in his dressing room. Aware of his reputation, I told him about NBC's policy regarding drug humor. Everything was fine, all very friendly. Dress rehearsal, no problem. Then came the air show — different story. All of a sudden Sam is ranting about how the drug war has dried up the pot supply:

> The drug war's on. They've got the pot. The pot's gone...
> You know it's true. They've got the pot, man.
> Now they want everybody to stop smoking crack, y'know
> Please stop smoking crack.
> Please stop smoking crack.
> OK, we'll make you a deal. We'll stop smoking crack if you give us the pot back!
> We'll trade you the crack for the pot.
> We'll trade you the crack for the pot!

Sam told me later he resorted to this stuff because he was "dying" onstage. I was doing the same watching from the control room. It didn't help that he also threw in a bit about the last word uttered by Jesus as he was nailed to the cross — "Ahgggh!"

Off I scurried to Engineering to make sure these blasphemies were edited from the delayed version that airs in the western time zones. And I believe we set a Guiness Book of World Records entry for the longest bleep in television history. This was followed by a letter from Broadcast Standards to the Program Department "asking" that Kinison not be invited to guest on *Saturday Night Live* again. Fat chance. Show business being the highly moral enterprise that it is, Kinison was rewarded for his lies and bad behavior with a lot of free publicity — "Network Censors Comedian!" — which in turn brought him

119

an invitation to <u>host</u> SNL a few weeks later, a decision that thrilled the Broadcast Standards Department not at all. When I saw Sam that week, he apologized for his past behavior and I shrugged it off. No sense in getting into a fight about it, although I would have loved to tell him to his face what a liar he was. Hopefully, he was contrite and would stay on his best behavior. Therefore, I was pleased to get a call from producer Lorne Michaels, asking me to review a routine Sam wanted to perform.

Not quite trusting Sam altogether, nor myself, I brought my boss, Rick Gitter, to Lorne's office where we were privileged to witness Sam's portrayal of a homosexual necrophiliac in the act of having sex. Sam played both parts, rolling around on the carpet. Rick and I found it difficult to believe what we were seeing.

I should interject here that the practice of taking a look at how material plays is a fairly common one in the censor business. You learn after a while that material often seems more offensive on paper than it does in performance. Bernadette Peters, for example, once wanted to sing a ballad called "Making Love Alone." It was exactly what it sounded like, a paean to the joys of masturbation:

> "There's a special kind of bliss
> Not engendered by a kiss
> Surreptitiously indulged in
> Less well known
> For when one cannot make love with another
> One can still make love alone"

Naturally we were concerned when we saw the lyrics, but the writers insisted we had to see Bernadette actually do the piece. We went to the Green Room for an audition. She was playing it straight, as a torch singer standing by a piano, dressed in a formal gown. Very elegant, no suggestive gestures, beautifully sung. We let it on the air.

Sam Kinison, needless to say, was no Bernadette Peters. We rejected his homosexual necrophiliac routine with barely a pretense of thinking it over. Sam protested, Sam's manager protested and Lorne Michaels protested. "Get me Brandon!" Lorne ordered, referring to NBC Entertainment President Brandon Tartikoff. This was one of Lorne's favorite ploys. The moment we said no to anything, he was on the phone to Brandon, asking him to talk us into changing our minds. Lorne must have tried this technique a thousand times, but I can't ever remember it working. In Kinison's case, though, I have to believe that even Lorne didn't really expect it to. He was merely putting on a show of outrage for the benefit of his host. That was something else I learned: no producer ever agreed with Standards in front of his stars.

Sam didn't go on live TV that Saturday without our taking the precaution of instituting a seven-second taped delay, only the second time in the history of *SNL* such a delay was used. The first was for Richard Pryor in 1976. (It would be used again in 1990 for Andrew Dice Clay.) The problem with the tape delay is that it doesn't work. First of all, the show must begin production seven seconds before 11:30, with a videotape running through a looping device that transmits the show seven seconds later. An editor sits in a tiny room somewhere in the bowels of NBC, watching the show on a monitor, waiting for something that has to be bleeped. When he hears it, he signals a technician who counts off seven seconds while the tape loop runs through an editing machine to precisely the point at which the obscenity occurred. Then he hits the "zap" button. Such timing is guesswork, and with the comedian talking fast and with all the crowd noise, misses are more frequent than hits. Sure enough, after Kinison's show that night I was on my way to engineering, hurrying to bleep Sam's random obscenities.

I always hoped that any Broadcast Standards message, quietly but firmly delivered with a minimum amount of screaming, yelling (and sobbing) would be effective and that everyone would behave. At 11:30 PM I prayed a lot, but the cast regulars and several hundred guest hosts, less the Kinisons and Rockets, were totally professional.

Perhaps I owe a debt of gratitude to Charlie Rocket after all. He didn't have his contract renewed and I suspect the performers who followed him were reminded of his indiscretion. I was always fond of Charlie but disappointed that he never apologized personally. I took a lot of heat, but I kept my job and he lost his, so it balances out. What a surprise.

And while there was no connection, the Sam Kinison story had a tragic ending when Sam, newly married and drug free after many years of abuse, I'm told, was killed in a horrific traffic accident on his way to Las Vegas. Sam was a bad boy but could charm the balls off a monkey and certainly didn't deserve such a rotten and early death.

It is appalling that naked women
Cannot be kept out of the nation's living rooms.
— **Billy Graham**, 1970

Statistics have told us that the largest number of viewer complaints about *SNL* regarded material associated with death. High on the list, for example, was a News Update joke at the time actress Claudine Longet killed her lover, skier Spider Sabich. Announced as coverage of the "Claudine Longet Invitational" ski tournament, a skier was seen careening down the slope, there was a gunshot, and he fell out of control. Then there was a tasteless item called "Kill Gary Gilmore" in which the cast sang a special Christmas carol, "Kill Gary Gilmore for Christmas," an anti-death penalty satire. But the most angry (and justifiable) response was an infamous piece, supposedly showing the funeral procession of recently assassinated gay San Francisco Supervisor Harvey Milk, gagged up with stock news footage of a horde of Chinese soldiers identified as either "dominant" or "submissive," paying homage.

The trick, if there is one, is to withhold humor about death and/or natural tragedies for an appropriate period of time. The safest path, of course, is to not do such jokes at all, something anathema to the writers of *SNL*.

The second most objected-to category was religion, and do we have the scars to prove it! Catholics, Jews, Muslims, Protestants — we heard from all of them. The only group not heard from was the Amish, only because they don't watch television.

Way back in 1945, NBC promulgated the following policy regarding religion:

"DEITY: The use of the deity's name, or reference to His powers and attributes, is permissible only when used reverently.

CREED: Statements and suggestions which ridicule or deride religious views, creeds and customs are prohibited.

SACRAMENTS: Baptism, marriage, burial and other sacraments and ceremonials must be treated with good taste and accuracy whenever they are referred to.

MINISTERS; Ministers of religion represented in their calling shall not be presented as undesirable characters or to be made the subject of amusement."

Got that, Father Sarducci?

Strange as it may seem, the good Father, as portrayed by comedian Don Novello, was so sweet and positive in his persona that he caused little consternation in the religious community. I've always suspected that the Catholic Church was secretly delighted to be so humanized.

Great pains were made, however, to assure that sacred rites such as communion, confession or the resurrection were not lampooned. Not that mistakes didn't occur and lines of proper respect crossed. Certainly no one could have misunderstood Sam Kinison's scream as he pretended to be Jesus having nails driven into his hands.

Then there were rejected gems such as "Towels of Turin."

OPEN ON ART CARD OF SHROUD OF TURIN WITH JESUS' FACE.
MUSIC: HOLY MONASTIC MUSIC

HARRY (VOICEOVER)

The miracle of the Shroud of Turin. For centuries the image of our Lord Jesus Christ has mysteriously remained on this ancient cotton cloth. Now, you and your family can enjoy the inspiring beauty of our Savior's face.

DISSOLVE TO: TOWEL HANGING ON TOWEL RACK IN BATHROOM
…with the Towels of Turin collection.

WIDEN TO REVEAL THE WHOLE RACK OF TOWELS, OF DIFFERENT SIZES, FROM BATH TO WASHCLOTH, EACH WITH THE SAME FAMOUS IMAGE.

...100% cotton, the Towels of Turin add comfort, durability and piety to your bathroom.

PAULA STEPS OUT OF SHOWER WEARING BATH TOWEL

PAULA (PRENTISS)

I like the soft, comfortable feel of a 100% cotton Towel of Turin, and I like the way it looks. And so does my husband! (WALKS TO TOWEL RACK AND POINTS TO DIFFERENT TOWELS, DISPLAYING THEM LIKE A MODEL)

(MUSIC: TURN, TURN, TURN)

JONI MITCHELL-TYPE VOICE

For every purpose—Turin, Turin, Turin
There is a washcloth—Turin, Turin, Turin
And a towel—for every need
In your bathroom

***

No, boys, no. Yet a few years later the following was approved:

OPEN ON BRIAN AS REVEREND JERRY FALWELL STANDING NEAR A GAUDY HOME ENTERTAINMENT UNIT/STEREO SURROUNDED BY SIGNS OF HIS RELIGIOUS STANDING. CHYRON SUPER: "REVEREND JERRY FALWELL"

BRIAN

Parents, are you troubled by the moral decay rampant among today's teenagers? Hello, I'm Reverend Jerry Falwell. Have you ever wondered what your young people are listening to on those tiny headphones of theirs? I can assure you it's not our Master's Voice. No, sir. It's the secret stereophonic whisperings of Satan! How many times have we seen a youngster listen to a rock and roll recording and then talk back to his parents, and fornicate. Never forget that it's only a short skip from a phonograph needle to the hypodermic needle. Rock and Roll is the Devil's music — until now. Because for just $9.98 you can now use this same music to deliver your children from evil. It's all here in my new born again rock and roll collection, "Jesus in Blue Jeans." (HOLDS UP ALBUM) You get 24 great rock hits, but no sex and no drugs, just good rockin' love songs to God.

ROLL VIDEOTAPE SEQUENCE OF PHOTOS WITH THE FOLLOWING MUSIC

HELP ME, RHONDA
IT'S MY PARTY
MY BOYFRIEND'S BACK
YUMMY, YUMMY, YUMMY
BABY LOVE

BRIAN

Ah...my Lord, that's righteous music. If you love your children, just send me $9.98 in care of this station. But remember, the Lord works in mysterious ways, so allow four to six weeks for delivery. And if you act now, we'll send you absolutely free a one-year subscription to "All Along the Watchtower" magazine. (HOLDS UP COVER WHICH RESEMBLES THE RELIGIOUS

PUBLICATION BUT WITH A LONG-HAIRED GUITAR PLAYER ON COVER)

So send for my record today — or burn in hellfire eternal.

(CHYRON CRAWL OVER PRETAPE)

HELP ME, JESUS
BORN AGAIN TO BE WILD
(LET'S GET) METAPHYSICAL
SYMPATHY FOR THE SAVIOR
BROWNEYED HANDSOME GOD
MUSTANG JESUS
THE MESSIAH'S BACK
HAVE YOU SEEN THE SAVIOR, BABY
STANDING IN THE SHADOWS?
STAG O LORD
JESUS IS A PUNK ROCKER
50 WAYS TO LOVE YOUR SAVIOR
(I CAN'T GET NO) RESURRECTION
SHORT SHORTS
HOUND GOD
JESUS WAS A ROLLING STONE
WHY DON'T WE GET DRUNK AND PRAY
MACHO GOD
THE YELLOW ROSARY OF TEXAS
RED RUBBER GOD
HOLY GHOST RIDERS IN THE SKY
JESUS JESUS KO-KO-BOP

We edited out "I can't get no Resurrection" and "Red Rubber God" for some reason already forgotten, but otherwise it ran as written.

There were scattered complaints about "Jesus in Blue Jeans," which we'd approved as a legitimate spoof on the over-commercialization of religion by certain broadcast preachers, without being sacrilegious. The target was not religion, but the corruption of it. As always, there were those who either misunderstood — or chose not to understand. But why did we approve "Jesus in Blue Jeans" and not "Towels of Turin?" Part of the reason was subjective. There was something so intrinsically tasteless about a bath towel containing the image of Christ being used to dry one's body. Too, there was audience expectation regarding *SNL*'s humorous and satirical approach. Whatever the reason, "Towels of Turin" was merely a cheap shot searching for a quick laugh, while "Jesus in Blue Jeans" was an acceptable sketch with satirical validity. There is no record of Reverend Falwell's reaction.

The Pope has been represented on occasion, not without criticism by the Archdiocese of New York, although they are unaware of the many times that material demeaning to the Church was rejected. For example, there was a sketch based on gays in the military, set in a barracks, its pinup picture not Christie Brinkley, but Terence Cardinal Cooke! We had it replaced with a photo of, I believe, Judy Garland.

A couple of times we spoofed Pope John Paul II's traveling, especially the commercial aspects of his trips. In one skit, His Holiness (Joe Piscopo) was portrayed as a sort of Borscht Belt comic tap dancing his way through Africa, accompanied by a sleazy agent-like bishop (Eddie Murphy!). The comedy had been inspired by a *PEOPLE* magazine article:

"POPEPOURRI: Pope John Paul II, back from Africa, will be paying a visit to England this May, and some of the same entrepreneurs who cashed in on last summer's royal wedding are readying an assortment of commemorative bowls, portraits, books, and even teaspoons. Other items approved by Mark McCormack's International Management Group, the Vatican's souvenir clearing-house, include special papal bricks, beer coasters, plastic bags and busts and a $2400 platinum medal with John Paul II's likeness on one side and the Queen's on the other. All this may smack of crass

129

commercialism, but at least these folks have some standards. Dozens of proposals were vetoed because the products were poorly made or would, by their very nature, get soiled (i.e., aprons, doormats and tea towels.) Also rejected were 'papal perfume' and lollipops bearing His Holiness' official logo."

The knowledge that Mark McCormack had rejected tea towels and aprons not only validated our decision to turn down "Towels of Turin," but the overall tackiness validated the papal visit to England as proper fodder for the satirist.

Incidentally, most of those papal items are still on sale at the Vatican gift shops, including a Pope John Paul II bottle opener. I know, for Don Novello showed me one. The Vatican is inspiring — The Sistine Chapel, The Pieta, the Vatican Museum — but it can be less than upscale. I attended an outdoor audience with 35,000 other pilgrims one summer's day, continually accosted by a string of hawkers selling papal coins, rosaries and other souvenirs for blessing by the Holy Father.

The Pope had been vacationing at Castel Gondolfo and would be flying in for the audience. While we waited, the huge throng sweating it out in St. Peter's Square was entertained by a tiny Italian army band and a priest who acted as a sort of emcee, recognizing the many groups in attendance. An expectant cry went up as the Pope's helicopter appeared right on schedule, circled the crowd, then landed behind St. Peter's. The crowd waited his entrance expectantly. In a few minutes, the Popemobile entered the plaza, a great cry went up and the band struck up entrance music. And to what reverent and stirring accompaniment does a Polish pope enter? Why, what else? The *Beer Barrel Polka!*

No matter how careful we were with comedic presentations involving religion, it was at best an uncomfortable mix and, from our point of view, a no-win situation. For example, we okayed a piece called "Pagan Easter" that had a bunch of trolls, satyrs and other disreputable blue-faced types dancing around and carrying on in a less than temperate fashion. It brought upon us this curse:

"...a sketch blaspheming the Holy Name of the Living God of Jews and Christians. You, your writers, your producers, your actors and anyone else associated with the airing of this show have willfully accepted the responsibility and guilt associated with this act. How can you answer for this audacity when you will ultimately stand before the very Throne of this Living God?

However, the God of the Israelites and Christians is merciful and I admonish you and all your associates to review this program, determine your guilt and collectively and privately throw yourself on his mercy while you still have time. Search your Scriptures and see for yourself the result of blasphemy forgiven. Act accordingly!"

Believe it or not, we took even such far-out criticism seriously. While we felt the writer had over-reacted, we replied in kind, thanks to the good office of NBC's religious advisor who helped us frame the following response:

"The Pagan Easter Celebration about which you complained was reviewed, as are all skits on *Saturday Night Live* by NBC's Broadcast Standards editors. This is no easy task, I assure you, since the nature of this show is satirical and irreverent. It's what we call 'an equal opportunity offender,' having outraged Protestants, Catholics, Jews, Muslims, Atheists, Gays, Women's Liberation, national political figures, most vocations, leading American corporations and not least of all, NBC/RCA/GE, the hand that feeds them.

Obviously a different standard is used for a late night satire than on the *Bill Cosby Show*. A key moral question is: what truth, if any, lies behind the targets they hit? In this case, the writers (having been discouraged from any direct reference to Christianity) seized upon the undoubted fact that Christians 'borrowed' Easter from the pagans....the Christian feast of Easter has superceded an old Pagan festival...according to Bede, it is connected with an Anglo-Saxon spring goddess, 'Eostre.' (cf. Oxford Dictionary of the Christian Church, p. 437.) With this in mind, the writers sought to create an original pagan Easter, thought of a spring fertility rite. Since this had nothing to do with the Resurrection, not alluding to Christianity at all, we felt it was within the boundaries of outrageous satire. The target was not Christians but pagans. And by pagans it was clear from the reference to Las Vegas, rock groups and Ivan Boesky, that these 'believers were consistent in their worship of Mammon'. Believe me, the editors would not have passed this skit if they thought it was aimed at Christian belief."

How's that for covering one's ass — by quoting Bede! And putting Bede and Ivan Boesky in the same paragraph!

Without question, the biggest flap over religion involved a sketch in 1979 called "Nerd's Nativity" and I was in the middle of it. The situation was hilariously documented in the best-selling book, *Saturday Night,* an historical (and hysterical) overview of the first five years of *Saturday Night Live,* written by talented writers Doug Hill and Jeff Weingrad. They've graciously permitted me to reprint their description of "Nerd's Nativity," but please, don't make me read it again, it's too painful

"*Saturday Night's* greatest Standards battle ever unfolded the week of December 22, 1979. The sketch at issue was called the 'Nerd's Nativity.' It featured Nerds Lisa Loopner and Todd DiLaMuca, played by Gilda Radner and Bill Murray, two of the show's most popular characters. It was written, as almost all of the Nerds sketches were, by Anne Beatts and Rosie Shuster. Lorne wanted something Christmassy for the show, so they had the Nerds performing in a high school nativity pageant. An innocent enough idea on the surface, but Standards didn't see it that way.

As soon as the Standards editor, Bill Clotworthy, read the piece on Wednesday, he raised a red flag with his boss, Ralph Daniels. Daniels had recently taken over Herminio Traviesas' job when Travie, semi-retired, moved into a corporate policy position, Clotworthy himself had only been a censor for a few weeks. *Saturday Night* was his first assigned show.

Clotworthy and Daniels didn't care for a joke in the sketch that had Todd describing Lisa as one of the few girls in school who was "physically correct" for the part of the Virgin Mary, nor were they amused when one of the Wise Men gestured at Joseph's mule (played by Alan Zweibel) and said, 'Get your ass out of here.' But more than that, they were bothered by the whole concept: It seemed to them to be satirizing one of Christianity's most sacred events, the birth of Christ. Not a good idea, they thought, especially three days before Christmas. Daniels flatly rejected the piece. 'The nativity is central to an entire religion,' he told Lorne. 'You cannot spoof the nativity.'

Lorne argued that what was being spoofed was not the nativity but high school nativity pageants, where the wise men wore bathrobes, the star of Bethlehem was made of tinfoil, and the holy family had paper plates pinned to their heads for halos. 'I went to that school!' he said. He kept the piece in production, suggesting, as he often had in the past, that Standards ought at least to see how it came across in dress rehearsal.

Daniels wasn't negotiating. He'd watched Travie deal with *Saturday Night Live* for several years and was of the opinion that Michaels & Co. had been getting away with far more than they should have. The show by then was a huge success at a time when NBC had very few successes. It seemed to Daniels that everybody at NBC had the attitude that, as he put it, 'these guys can do pretty much what they want.' He decided it wasn't going to be that way under his Standards department, and the 'Nerds Nativity' sketch was where he drew the line. Daniels refused even to discuss it.

Lorne, by then used to winning his fights with Standards, was every bit as adamant. The sketch, with some of the racier lines removed, played in dress rehearsal on Saturday. Afterward Lorne told Bill Clotworthy and Josh Kane, an NBC program executive who was brought in to help mediate, 'The sketch is staying in the show. You can do what you want.'

That didn't leave NBC with many pleasant alternatives. They could take the whole show off the air and put on a rerun. They could run a videotaped sketch from an earlier show over the Nerds sketch when it went on. Or, as Josh Kane later joked, they could bring armed guards into the studio and have them stand in front of the set. Any of these choices would result, they knew, in the very public resignation of the producer. At that point, Kane said, 'the race was on.'

Between dress and air, Clotworthy and Lorne were on the phone in Lorne's ninth-floor office with Cory Dunham (Head of NBC's Law Department) and Ralph Daniels. Lorne tried to enlist the aid of Mike Weinblatt, (NBC Program VP) who was at the show, but Weinblatt deferred to Daniels's judgment. Daniels was talking from a phone booth in a restaurant, and he wasn't happy about talking at all. There was a lot of shouting, but Daniels was softening his position enough to begin to discuss some of the lines that would have to be cut if they were to let the sketch on.

As they talked, Josh Kane was rushing to NBC's videotape archives with a unit manager to look for a sketch of similar length to run over the 'Nerds Nativity' if it came to that. They found a suitable sketch and gave it to the engineer in central control, telling him to stand by.

Meanwhile the advertising reps covering the show had seen the 'Nerds Nativity' sketch in dress. Most of them didn't want their clients' spots anywhere near it. Uncertain of whether it would be on the air show, several of the reps decided that discretion was the better part of valor and told NBC's ad rep, Sue Schwartz, they wanted out of the show. Schwartz, realizing the company was about to lose an unprecedented 40 percent or more of its revenue for the night, decided to break all the rules and started looking for a program executive to plead that the sketch should not be put on. She couldn't find anyone, so she called her boss, Robert Conrad, at home. Conrad's solution was simple. He instructed Schwartz to tell the agencies NBC refused to take them out of the show. Some of the ad reps found that hard to believe.

'I'm telling you we're not paying for the unit,' one of them yelled at Schwartz, 'and I've gone on record as demanding to be out of the show!' The calls and the shouting between the reps, Conrad, Schwartz, and various agency executives continued as the show went on the air.

Anne Beatts was in the ladies' room at 11:28 when somebody pounded on the door, shouting at her to get to Lorne's office. As she arrived, Lorne raced out saying, 'Bill Clotworthy's in there—go talk to him!' Beatts, who had been uncertain all week what would happen with the sketch, was bewildered: She thought the 'Nerds Nativity' was supposed to be the second sketch in the show, which meant it should be going on in minutes. She

135

didn't know Lorne had moved it back to just after midnight to gain some time. Rosie Shuster came in, and she could see the show in progress on the monitor in Lorne's office as she and Beatts argued with Daniels on the phone.

'You can't say the word *ass*,' Daniels told them.

"We've used the word before," Beatts protested.

'Not in front of Mary and Joseph, you haven't,' Daniels replied.

Daniels also wanted a piece of business cut in which Bill Murray's Todd rubbed his knuckles affectionately across the head of Gilda's Lisa in a 'noogie attack.' Todd gave Lisa noogies in every Nerds sketch, and it always got a laugh, but Daniels wouldn't' hear of it in a nativity scene.

'You can't give noogies to the Virgin Mary!' he shouted at Beatts.

'But she's not the Virgin Mary!' Beatts shouted back. 'She's Gilda Radner playing Lisa Loopner playing the Virgin Mary with a paper plate on her head!'

Beatts, Shuster, and three production assistants, Julia Fraser, Jeannine Kerwin, and Robin Shlein, ran the changes to cue cards and the control room just as the sketch was to go on the air. They only had time to tell the actors, 'Just read the cards. It's all different.'

The actors had some choice words in response to that, especially Bill Murray, who yelled at Beatts later, 'Don't you ever do that to me again!'

The sketch played fairly well on air, considering, but no one was really happy with it. Too many lines had been lost and too many egos bruised. Todd did, however, give Lisa her noogies that night.

The following Monday, Ralph Daniels wrote a memo to Cory Dunham saying Standards would no longer cover *Saturday Night*. If Standards made a ruling and Lorne Michaels ignored it, Daniels said, then what was the point? The memos' underlying message was clear: Either Dunham brought Michaels into line, or Daniels would quit.

Dunham called a meeting in his office that Wednesday. Attending were Lorne, Daniels, Clotworthy, Josh Kane, and Mike Weinblatt. Daniels repeated his conviction that Lorne's 'steamroller' approach had to stop. 'A producer cannot say, This stays in because I say it stays,' Daniels said. 'That's why we have a Standards department. If the producer is not willing to be flexible, and if it's his determination that something goes on, then I'm removing my people.'

Lorne repeated his defense of the sketch, but his tone was conciliatory. As Josh Kane saw it, Lorne could afford to be conciliatory at that point. At the end of the meeting everyone shook hands and agreed to try to work together more smoothly. Cory Dunham reflected later that an appropriate balance seemed to have been struck: Sometimes the producer wanted to resign because of Standards and sometimes Standards wanted to resign because of the producer.

As Daniels staged his protest, Robert Conrad in Sales was soothing the ruffled feathers of the agencies who had been forced to stay in the show. In the NBC mail room, stacks of letters were pouring in from viewers who wanted to know how *Saturday Night* could make fun of the baby Jesus."

Contrary to the book, there were not stacks of mail protesting the sketch, even though we expected plenty. Discounting Reverend Wildmon's organized campaign a few years later, "Nerds Nativity" didn't even come close to a record. Actually there were more complaints about one-time host Eric Idle's monologue featuring a slapstick routine with a live cat in his pants and Magician Harry Anderson's illusion wherein he appeared to eat a live guinea pig! Heck, we got over a hundred calls when Gilda did a little routine carrying her own docile, well-behaved cat. People called to complain that the cat was obviously drugged! These are the same folks, I suspect, who toss paint on fur coats, or sponsor full-page ads protesting the slaughter of dogs, cows lambs, parrots, snakes or the consumption of shellfish.

The most famous religious representation on SNL was, as you would expect, "The Church Lady," played by Dana Carvey in drag. She epitomized the strict, purse-lipped, stereotypical Christian spinster, and became a tremendous hit. She struck a responsive chord with the public, although it was often necessary to tone down her graphic descriptions of "male bulges" and "thrusting, heaving buttocks."

The Jews really deserve their own chapter. On one hand there was the "But Al's Jewish" perspective tempered by the very real problem of acceding to normal religious protection. And talk about déjà vu. As recently as December 16, 1999, SNL was criticized by the Anti-Defamation League of B'nai B'rith as described (in part) in the *Washington Post*:

> "NBC has promised the Anti-Defamation League of B'nai B'rith that it will never rebroadcast a recent *Saturday Night Live* sketch in which cast members, pretending to be pop stars, say that Jews own all the banks and that Christians have forgiven them for killing our Lord.
>
> At least that's what NBC said last week in a letter. Yesterday the official peacock word was 'We currently have it under review.' Meanwhile, SNL Executive producer Lorne Michaels told the TV Column that he's vehemently opposed to any guarantee the sketch won't run again and says that ADL 'trivializes the important work they're supposed to be doing with this kind of nonsense.'"

Apparently (I don't look at the show anymore) the sketch in question was a parody of a CBS Christmas Special called *So This is Christmas* that featured Celine Dion, Ricky Martin, Gloria Estefan and Britney Spears. SNL's take was *So This is Hanukah,* in which cast members impersonated Dion, Martin and Spears recalling their early Christmas memories when Hanukah is a holiday celebrated by the people who own all the movie studios and the banks; the time of year when we as Christians take time out to think about forgiving our Jewish friends for killing our Lord."

The *Washington Post* article went on to say that the ADL blasted the bit as representing "anti-Semitic stereotypes at their worst. To have Spears refer to forgiving Jews for 'having killed our Lord' is no laughing matter. We have worked with the Vatican and others for the last fifty years to educate against this poisonous doctrine and for *SNL*, in a lame attempt at humor, to revive this notion, is unacceptable."

In response, NBC assured the ADL that the problematic sketch would be excised from all future broadcasts. Now, I could have guaranteed a response to that edict from Lorne Michaels who was quoted by the *Post*, "After 25 years, people know that SNL is a satire. What satire is supposed to do is provoke discussion. We're not pro-drugs, but we make jokes about drugs; we're not pro-ignorance, but we make jokes about ignorance, and the only way you can do it by showing ignorance. The idea that any discussion of these ideas is out of bounds is idiotic to me."

Talk about "Here we go again."

1979. Internal: "A representative of the Jewish Defense League called to complain about the Superman skit...his position was that the sketch was not only offensive to Jewish people but incited anti-semitism and that his organization, therefore, felt it would have to 'do something' about it. This person expressly denied any intention of using violence but implied that others in his

organization did not share his views on the desirability
of restraint."

That was 1979, and the studio remained standing, but that
will give you an idea of how strongly some audience members
felt about some of the satire and stereotyping.

It was always a surprise to me, however, that Lorne
Michaels, Al Franken and a number of writers of the Jewish faith
would ever submit comedy material based on the Holocaust! I
mean, *Saturday Night Live* took a shot at everything including
child abuse and incest, but the Holocaust? None ever got on the
air, the closest being a sketch in 1984 called "Dutch Couple"
about a couple who had forgotten to release a family they'd
hidden in their attic from the Nazis during World War II. In that
case, most of the complaints were about Eddie Murphy playing a
Jew!

The function of the censor is to censor. He has a
professional interest in finding things to suppress.

— Thomas I. Emerson

I don't like to be called a censor because that just means
saying no. I like to say — let's find a better way of
doing it.

— Herminio Traviesas

Speaking of thrusting buttocks (which we were, earlier), the craziest and most irreligious adventure I approved was Uncle Elmer's wedding on *Saturday Night's Main Event*, the wrestling extravaganza that replaced *SNL* on occasion. As a matter of fact, I was party to the event, much to my shame. Uncle Elmer was a WWF wrestler, a 400-pound hillbilly whose gimmick was wearing bib overalls, a floppy hat and a gentle, sweet nature. Elmer was no kid, just a sweet middle-aged man with diabetes and other problems, trying to make a living before his time ran out. His partner was his nephew, Hillbilly Jim, who, when Elmer was being tossed around, came to his rescue by swatting the bad guys with a 2 by 4. What a great sport.

Elmer made the mistake of announcing his engagement and the geniuses behind *Saturday Night's Main Event* thought it would be clever to have Elmer marry in the ring on national television, and he agreed. The producers, Dick Ebersol and Vince MacMahon (Mr. Class) asked for our approval and advice. Harking back to Tiny Tim's wedding to Miss Vicky, we couldn't conjure up a reason not to proceed and I even suckered our religious advisor, Dr. Richard Gilbert, into writing the ceremony although he wisely opted not to personally officiate.

On the big night an arbor was set up in the ring, Uncle Elmer, best man Hillbilly Jim and a local minister were in place, and the radiant bride, a waitress from Tennessee, marched down the aisle and up into the ring — now, there was a pretty sight; a bride in a wedding gown clambering between ring ropes. What we had not been told, however, was that wrestler Rowdy Roddy Piper and a couple of henchmen were to be disruptive by tossing golf balls, batteries and other junk at the bride and groom, to make snide and insulting comments and otherwise break up the ceremony in the name of television "entertainment." In proper wrestling mode, of course, Hillbilly Jim leaped to Elmer's defense by starting a fracas with Piper that turned into a less-than-romantic experience in the married life of Mr. and Mrs. Uncle Elmer.

I attended a number of wrestling specials that were clearly identified at the insistence of the Law Department as "entertainment," although I've often wondered about the entertainment value of such a "sport." The wrestlers themselves were friendly, interesting and even charming; it was the audience that was nuts. It was depressing to watch youngsters who actually believed the patently ridiculous and scripted bouts — screaming and yelling and, worst of all, being taught at an impressionable age that violence is a means to an end. I am not moved by the argument that the entertainment aspect of wrestling obviates its influence on tender minds. I've seen the looks on those faces. I was delighted when NBC ended its love affair with professional wrestling. (Author's note: The press reports that NBC has entered into a partnership with Vince McMahon and his new football league which promises to be more violent and hard-hitting than the present NFL. No protection for the quarterback, no fair catches, etc. Sounds just like wrestling to me.)

Of course, wrestling is still all over the tube, primarily in syndication and local programming. I've often wondered why the fools on the Hill haven't investigated professional wrestling. Its message of violence, sexual harassment and other sins is clear. Senators?

Violence was not a problem on *Saturday Night Live*, thank goodness, unless one considered its humor an assault on common sense. I've my own opinion about the harm to young minds from the plethora of violence on television, but except trying to contain the worst of it in a feature film already shot, I had little control. By the way, if you don't think there's much violence on television, play a little game called "Find the Gun," which can be played at almost any time, including Sundays. Channel surf at your leisure and I guarantee you'll find at least one scene that includes a gun, knife or violence. At any time of the day or night.

As I wrote this (A Tuesday afternoon) I tried it and found four. The first was a promo for *Cops* in which they pounded down a door and swarmed into a room with guns drawn. Next was a promo for, of all things, a soap opera, in which two characters plotted the killing of another. Then came a Kris Kristofferson movie in which a sheriff waved his gun around followed by a movie on *Lifetime* in which a middle-aged woman with a rifle ran into a house.

Then I tried it later, at 8 PM, still the so-called "family hour", named, I think, in honor of the Manson Family. This time I found only three. The first was a film in which one guy called another an "arrogant son of a bitch" over the phone, then a girl entered, threw herself on the guy, wrapping her legs around him before rolling onto the bed. Before consummation, however, she exited, enabling another guy to enter and graphically shoot the first guy. Having enough, I switched to a Western just in time to watch a man killed in cold blood in the street, then watch his corpse dragged away behind the killer's horse.

Well, you get the idea. Violence, threats to bodily harm, knives and guns are ubiquitous. And this is the entertainment shows, I haven't even mentioned the News! Mores 's the pity. For our nation.

I don't think pornography is very harmful
But it is very, very boring.

— Noel Coward

The Plaza Hotel in Hollywood was the gathering spot for horse players waiting for the bus to Hollywood Park or Santa Anita. Ex-Fighter Slapsie Maxie Rosenbloom and stuttering comedian Joe Frisco were among the daily habitues. My friend Dick Dwan and I passed by one day and Joe Frisco, thinking he knew us, said hello. Dick stopped and said, "Oh, you don't know me, Mr. Frisco. My name is Dick Dwan. I'm from Burlingame." Frisco, without missing a beat, replied, "Oh, I know where B-b-b-Burlingame is. It's between T-t-t-Tanforan and B-b-b-Bay Meadows!" He was right, but only a true horse player would associate places in relationship to race tracks!

Which brings us to the motion picture, *A Fish Called Wanda,* the subject of controversy since the character played by comedian Eric Idle stuttered. Many felt it held the affliction up to ridicule. Idle responded that his father had been a stutterer and that no offense was intended. It did, however, raise the question of physical or emotional infirmity and whether those problems are fair game for satire or proper subjects for comedy. NBC's policy, and my personal feeling, was that they are not, which means that "Stutterin' Joe" Frisco would probably not work very much in television. And Foster Brooks' drunk act faded as we began to realize the severity of alcoholism as a national ailment.

Comedian Damon Wayans was hired by *SNL* as the token black after Eddie Murphy's departure. He was not successful on *SNL,* partially caused by creative conflicts with producer Lorne Michaels, although he went on to great fame on *In Living Color*. Damon prepared a monologue in which he portrayed a crippled ghetto character who walked with a severe limp. I felt the characterization was demeaning to the infirm and told Damon so. He replied that he'd had a club foot as a child and was sensitive to the problem. Unfortunately we cannot flash an advisory — "The performer had a club foot as a child and means no harm to those so afflicted" — we must interpret what the audience will perceive, and rejected the action. Damon disregarded our instructions and performed it, which meant yet another trip to the editing machines.

146

We missed once in a while, though. Host Steve Martin brilliantly spoofed *The Elephant Man* with a funny makeup job featuring a dangling elephant trunk in place of his nose. Unbeknownst to us, there are thousands of people in this country afflicted with neurofibromatosis and they were not amused. What can you do except plead ignorance, and apologize?

We were sharp enough to reject the following masterpiece, however, a head-shaker that made you wonder why it even left the typewriter:

JIM (AS A PITCHMAN)

Hello there, Christmas shoppers, this is your old holiday friend Fast Eddie with a Christmas offer that's so unique, so timely, that you will think you're actually in the news. Yes, I know you've all heard about those cute imported Cabbage Patch dolls, and many of you have probably tried to buy one, but with no luck. Well, here's just the thing for every young boy and girl on your Christmas list. That's right, just in time for Christmas, direct from Long Island, Fast Eddie is offering the very unique, very one of a kind...(HOLDS UP A BADLY BENT DOLL) Baby Jane Doe Doll. Yes, Baby Doe, just as much in the news as the imported Cabbage Patch kind, but Baby Doe is American conceived and American made: a true American issue. Why, even President Reagan and the federal government has one of these to help them get involved and show they care. But, best of all, when you give a Baby Doe Doll to your youngster you will have the confidence of knowing that it is a unique, one of a kind gift because, believe me, there won't be another kid on the block with a doll that looks like this. (HOLDS UP DOLLS BEING MENTIONED) We have Baby Doe hydrocephalics, Baby Doe spinal deformities, Baby Doe hole in the heart dolls and Baby Doe just plain what-the-hell-is-it dolls. And each Baby Doe doll comes with its own adoption papers so you and your child can face the same moral and medical dilemma that says all babies are cute and lovable. Get America's own reality doll...Baby Doe...available in five colors and nine denominations..."(FADE)

***

Ugh!

For people in the communications business, we often had a tough time communicating, witness a continuing problem with our understanding of schizophrenia. It began with a quip by David Letterman:

"Shocking story from Brooklyn: a schizophrenic was apparently the victim of a murder-suicide pact with himself."

Talk about timing. At that very moment, the National Alliance for the Mentally Ill (NAMI) was meeting in convention in Boston where many delegates heard the joke, reported it to their leaders, and a few days later we received over 800 letters written on the same hotel's stationery! NAMI represents the parents and other family members of the 2 million Americans who suffer from schizophrenia, concerned with not only finding a cure, but seeking the eradication of the stigma caused by misrepresentation of mental illness by the media.

Their letters provoked a series of meetings, lessons really, in which we were the students, learning about schizophrenia, its prevalence and danger signs. Most important, we were taught what it was not — and that is a split personality subject to humor.

I sent a note to Barry Sand, David Letterman's producer:

"Each time we make what we consider to be light-hearted fun of mental illness, we are negatively touching those who are afflicted with, or live with persons suffering from this condition. Schizophrenia, for example, is a mental disorder affecting over two million Americans, caused by a biochemical disturbance of the brain. Persons with schizophrenia do not have a 'split personality' and are not prone to criminal violence. We hope, therefore, that you will pass on to your staff the seriousness of this concern. We appreciate that there is no intent to demean persons with this disability. Yet, as we do not poke fun at those with cancer, MS, CP, blindness and other infirmities, neither should we be using any form of mental illness for humorous purposes."

Somehow that wise admonition was not communicated to our office in Burbank, however, resulting in a Robert Klein parody poem recited on the *Tonight Show*:

> "Roses are red
> Violets are blue
> I'm schizophrenic
> And so am I."

That goof was shortly followed by a line in *Highway to Heaven:*

> "A guy walks into a psychiatrist's office and says, 'I'm schizophrenic' and the doctor replies, 'that makes four of us.'"

NAMI was properly indignant about our stupidity, but we at last learned our lesson as evidenced by production of an outstanding *Movie of the Week*, "Strange Voices," starring Nancy McKeon, a film that showed the impact of schizophrenia on a family; the difficulty of finding medical service and, in particular, understanding from the community. The Broadcast

Standards Department, on behalf of the network, was proud to accept NAMI's prestigious Outstanding Public Education Through Television Award for "Strange Voices" at a national convention.

Censorship is the ultimate blasphemy
— **Michael Rubenstein**

Over the years, *Saturday Night Live* tackled a number of controversial subjects — gays in the military, incest, the death penalty, abortion and euthanasia, but none caused more dialogue than "First, He Cries," a sketch about cancer and mastectomy based on Betty Rollins' best-selling book, *First, You Cry,* that described her ordeal with breast cancer. The sketch, however, told the story from the male viewpoint, with Bill Murray playing a whining husband complaining about "his" loss, living with a "deformed freak," marriage to "Miss Uni-Boob" and other indignities. The point of the piece was the insensitivity and selfishness of the man, and the general male breast fetish in this country.

The payoff was that he finally realized that, despite the loss of a breast, he loved his wife and that she was still a complete human being. It started out like this:

OPEN IN DOCTOR'S OFFICE. BILLY AND GILDA ARE MEETING WITH DOCTOR (HOST BEA ARTHUR)

BEA
Mr. and Mrs. Anderson, I'm afraid that the biopsy came out positive.

GILDA
Then you'll have to perform a mastectomy?

BEA
That's right.

BILL
You mean cut off her breast?

BEA
I'm afraid so.

BILL

Why me?! God!? Why me?!
STING: SUPER OVER BILL: "FIRST, HE
CRIES." CUT TO CRAWL

PARDO (VO CRAWL)

The following docu-drama deals with a sensitive
social issue — mastectomy and its psychological effects,
not on the woman who undergoes the surgery, but on the
man in her life who must endure the anguish of living
with "half a woman."

***

Well, it went on and on, probably too long, with scenes in
the hospital room, at a party and back to the doctor's, all the time
Billy ranting about his marriage to a freak, then running off with
a sexy young bimbo before he meets with the doctor again:

BILL

…oh, the first couple of months with Bambi were
great. Especially the sex. And of course I'd never seen
Europe before. And the sex. But lately, I don't
know…she's so young. I mean she thinks the Beatles
were Paul McCartney's backup group. There's just not
much to talk to her about. There's…something missing.

BEA

Maybe that something is Irene.

BILL

But she's…she's half a woman.

BEA

Now, Larry, come on. (PULLS DOWN MEDICAL DIAGRAM SHOWING FEMALE PROFILE AND FRONT VIEWS)
What about the rear?

BILL

Well, yeah, right.

BEA

And the legs.

BILL

Yeah, well, I'll admit Irene has pretty nice gams.

BEA

OK! And how about the nape of the neck and the tummy. Don't forget those.

BILL

Yeah, I see what you mean. God, I can't believe I've been so blind. There's no real reason I can't enjoy sex with Irene and since we've known each other so long and have a family, we'd always have lots to talk about. If she'd only take me back!

BEA (PRESSING INTERCOM)

Irene, you can come in now.

BILL

You mean...?

BEA

Yes.
GILDA ENTERS, RUNS UP AND KISSES BILL

GILDA
Larry, I heard every word you said. I love you.

BILL
And I love you. (TAKES GILDA'S HAND AS HE OPENS THE DOOR, HE GRABS HER TUSH AND TURNS TO BEA) Thanks, Doc!
FREEZE FRAME.

***

Well, that script was presented to me about two weeks after my initiation with the "Nerds Nativity," but I was smart enough to smell trouble and that meant only one thing — getting a higher opinion! Ralph Daniels was unavailable (probably nursing his wounds from "Nerds Nativity!") so I went to see his boss and my dear friend, the Vice-President for Standards, a lovely gentleman with the improbable name of Herminio Traviesas. He asked me to read the sketch, so I stood nervously pretending to be a doctor, a mastectomy patient and a crummy husband. "Travie" thought for a long moment before remarking that his own sister was at that moment in time undergoing cancer therapy and was not expected to live. However, he felt the material addressed a legitimate issue, and approved it. Host Bea Arthur had no reservations about performing in the sketch although her sister had undergone a mastectomy. There were mixed feelings within the SNL staff, the most vocal negative voice that of Bill Murray who was unhappy playing such a distasteful character.

But the sketch was produced, with little artistic success, as the studio audience seemed bewildered, laughing only at the obligatory tit jokes, half-heartedly at that. Some of the television audience, however, were not laughing at all, they were incensed over the tastelessness of "First, He Cries." Author Doug Hill has said that Bea Arthur received an outraged phone call late that

155

night (actually morning) from a viewer who had tracked her down to her hotel, a story I'd not heard before.

One person who was not offended was Betty Rollin, author of the work on which the sketch was based:

"Dear Lorne Michaels,

I just wanted you to know that I wasn't the slightest bit offended by "First, He Cries." I don't think it should matter at all. You have the right to satirize anything and the more unlikely the subject the better. While I'm at it, it occurs to me that you must get a lot of moaning and groaning from people who think this or that is gauche or awful or tasteless. I hope you don't let it get you down! You have create the funniest show on television and if you stuck within safe boundaries, you might be less offensive, but you'd surely be less amusing."

A few years after the flap over "First, He Cries," my own wife developed breast cancer and underwent chemotherapy, radiation and surgery, including mastectomy. I cannot tell you how many times over the next few years I recalled that comedy sketch, and heard its truth, loud and clear. I am convinced that its message was very helpful in understanding my wife's need and my subsequent tolerance and patience with the terrible burden placed on us.

That's what satirical comedy is — truth. Exaggerated to be sure, but truth nevertheless, a reflection of our foibles, excesses and attitudes. George S. Kaufman once said, "Satire is what closes on Saturday night," but *Saturday Night Live* has been on the air for twenty-five years in spite of (or because of) its ventures into tastelessness, irreverence and controversy. It's been on the cutting edge, pushing the envelope of inventive and progressive humor, and telling the truth. Frankly, I hope it stays on, pricking the conscience, greed and self-righteousness of our leaders — and ourselves.

Of course, our leaders have really caught it! From Chevy Chase's bumbling Gerald Ford to Dan Aykroyd's numbing Richard Nixon to Dana Carvey's flailing George Bush, *SNL* has skewered politicians to a fare-thee-well. I must admit that some of the characterizations have bothered me. As a full-fledged member of the conservative WASP community, I have a built-in respect for the presidency, no matter what the party and I winced when Jimmy Carter was portrayed as delivering the State of the Union address while suffering from hemorrhoids and I really had to hold my tongue with the characterization of Ronald Reagan as a wattled, senile old coot. After all, he was a personal friend of mine.

And poor Nancy Reagan got a bad rap, portrayed a couple of times as a boozy, offensive, demanding harridan. When son Ron hosted the show, we did a spoof of *Back to the Future,* a picture in which the mother was a closet alcoholic. Maybe okay for that character, but insulting, I thought, for the First Lady of the land. I'm surprised young Reagan agreed to participate. I hadn't seen "Skipper" since he was a child and he was shocked when I addressed him that way. Another sketch was a spoof of a dancing film, *Footloose,* in which he danced around in his underwear. I asked if he was comfortable doing it (After all, he was the son of the President!) and he laughed and said not to worry, he was wearing dancing tights.

Not to worry, but a heck of a lot of people phoned and wrote to complain. The most famous letter (one of *SNL's* favorites?) was from humorist Henry Morgan who was less than thrilled with the show:

> "...the program of February 8th was so unrelievedly shocking that it embarrassed me to think that it could be aired in my country. Yes, that's what I said, my country....since the reeking ordure of the creative department is matched by the ineptitude of the cast, one can conclude only that the network itself is on the hands of morons....One Lorne Michaels is the producer? Is he

157

related to the other TV Lorne…the one who also peddles dog food?…whoever is ultimately responsible for this tragic accumulation of filth is himself revolting…"

C'mon, Henry, how do you really feel?

I'm glad I asked Ron, however. I dropped a note to Nancy saying how much we'd all enjoyed Ron's appearance, and received a hand-written reply of warm graciousness for "making a mother's heart soar."

Hey, these are nice people, but I think that sometimes comedians forget that when they make jokes about personality, character, appearance and personal problems that beset all of us. Unfortunately there are too few Art Buchwalds, Mort Sahls and Mark Russells bringing dignity and courtesy to political satire. Jokes about Reagan's senility, Ford's clumsiness or Carter's proctology are cheap shots that, in my view, demean the Office of President. It was a losing battle as the comedian is protected by liberal libel laws as regards public figures. So I had to shut my mouth and endure vitriolic and just plain nasty comments about the men holding America's highest office.

At times the vitriol is evident, such as the time host Howard Hesseman "mooned" the President. We had difficulty approving it and in production it exceeded our worst fears. It was tasteless, disgusting, insulting, personal and, worst of all, unfunny. We took a lot of heat on that one, and we deserved it. It should not have run.

Then there are times when the personal politics of the regular cast show through, as witness an Eddie Murphy commentary in favor of a national holiday honoring Martin Luther King. The commentary was filled with negative references to President Reagan and a plea to send letters that Eddie planned to dump on the front lawn of the White House. That bit of nonsense didn't happen, but there were 6,000 replies of support that were forwarded to the White House. Just what they needed, another 6000 letters. While we may have agreed with the cause, it was, unfortunately, a personal political statement expressed out of character and should not have been allowed. Oops.

The United States has a long history of political nastiness and vitriol. Even George Washington took it on the chin after he'd left office; "Your farewell was fraught with incalculable evils to your country. Would to God you had retired to a private station years ago!" or "If ever a nation was debauched by a man, the American nation has been debauched by Washington."

Alexander Hamilton wasn't a fan of John Adams... "I should be deficient in candor were I to conceal the conviction, that he does not possess the talents adapted to the administration of government, and that there are great and intrinsic defects in his character which unfit him for the office of Chief Magistrate. He is petty, mean, egoistic, erratic, jealous-natured, and hot-tempered."

But perhaps no one took the blows as did Thomas Jefferson. *The Federalist* described him as "A mean-spirited, low-level fellow, the son of a half-breed Indian squaw, sired by a Virginia Mulatto father — raised wholly on hoe cake made of coarse-ground southern corn, bacon and hominy, with an occasional change of fricaseed bullfrog." And if that weren't enough, *The Hartford Courant* predicted this kind of Jefferson administration: "Murder, robbery, rape, adultery and incest will all be openly taught and practiced, the air will be rent with the cries of the distressed, the soil will be soaked with blood, and the nation black with crime."

And Bill Clinton thought he had it rough with Monica Lewinsky.

Nevertheless, such attacks are not necessarily right, and are further exacerbated and amplified by constant media coverage, particularly television, as every idiosyncrasy, bobble and pimple is piped into homes across the nation.

No girl was ever ruined by a book
— **Oliver Wendell Holmes**

Believe it or not, during my tenure, there were no lawsuits brought against *SNL*, although advertisers often jumped ship. And while the show was sometimes merciless in spoofing commercials, the only complaint I recall was from E. and J. Gallo who objected to a spot featuring Bill Murray as a bum in the gutter thanks to his consumption of Thunderbird wine.

However, in my twelve years as a network censor and twenty-five years before that as an advertising executive, I'd be hard-pressed to think of a situation more bizarre than Martha Raye's lawsuit against NBC and David Letterman. *Late Night with David Letterman* fell under my realm of responsibility as Director although my colleagues Jane Crowley and Jay Ottley covered the show routinely. There were few problems on the show as David was a sensitive self-editor, but no one saw this one coming.

You may recall Miss Raye's commercials for Polident Denture Adhesive in which she was introduced as "Martha Raye, actress and denture wearer." Well, David Letterman came up with the following one-liner: "I saw the most terrifying commercial on television last night featuring Martha Raye, actress and condom user..."

Hardly a candidate for the Humor Hall of Fame, but essentially harmless. Except to Miss Raye, or at least to her attorney who sent NBC a stinging letter claiming defamation of character, the joke implying to them that Miss Raye was sexually promiscuous, exposed to AIDS, engaged in deviant sexual behavior and played the dominant male role in a lesbian relationship.

Have I missed anything beside the logic of the attorney's argument?

In the first place, all we were doing was satirizing a well-known commercial. Secondly, Martha Raye, one of America's great clowns and respected performers was, at the time, a frail and ailing 70 year-old woman confined to a wheelchair. There wasn't a person in the world who would take the attorney's claims seriously.

Yet, due to everyone's deep respect for Martha Raye as a performer and humanitarian, David apologized on the air: "On March 5, during the show I made a joke in my opening remarks relating to actress Martha Raye. The joke referred to her as 'actress and condom user.' The joke was intended to be a goof on Miss Raye's commercials for denture products and was not intended to imply that she uses or has any reason to use condoms. My apologies to Miss Raye."

The last line had originally been "My apologies to her family, friends, fans and attorneys," but after due consideration, the last line was revised at the request of NBC's Law department. After all, we wouldn't want to offend the legal profession, even though sensitivity and consideration are words not found in any legal dictionary.

The apology, duly delivered, was not accepted. Miss Raye (or her representatives) rejected it as being delivered later in the show than the original, and felt it was delivered in a sarcastic and arrogant manner. Well, what then can an attorney do? Why, sue! For $50,000 in general damages and a mere $10 million in punitive damages. Eventually the suit was tossed, but not before we did $50,000 worth of extra work in pulling files, answering interregatories and the like, such as identified with a Demand for Preservation of Evidence. Evidence? For God's sake, it was a joke! Anyway, here are some of the things asked for:

1. Tape recordings of sources, informants, tipsters, stringers, and witnesses, their written statements, if any, and transcripts of those tape recordings, as pertain to any information that Martha Raye uses or does not use condoms.
2. Individual producer's, editor's, writer's or other person's typed or handwritten notes, compositions, or remarks concerning the use, anticipated use, form, anticipated form, or questions or concerns about the propriety or appropriateness of Letterman's remarks.

3.   A tape of the entire show, including all opening and closing credits.
4.   All outtakes, retakes, edits, looping, reshooting or oral presentations not broadcast or published, but which were a part of, connected with, used with, omitted from, or intended for possible use in the scene or sequence of the Letterman Show concerning Miss Raye.
5.   The cue cards, if any, containing reference to the remark, or its substance, as used on the show, and all drafts or modifications thereof.
6.   Logs or records of any employees as pertain to the production schedule of the taped episode listed and described in 4 above, and records of your production facilities in connection therewith, showing the dates or dates of writing or filming of the March 5 show, the date of receipt by NBC, and the air date.
7.   Researcher's notes, markings or notations, whether on or apart from draft or copy, whether in NBC's file, production company files or personal to the researchers, relating to the demographics of the David Letterman Show.
8.   All papers, magazines, articles or clippings, if any, involving or about Martha Raye for the last five years, and all biographical publications in your library pertaining to her.
9.   All documents or writings pertaining to any conference, meeting, discussion, conversation, or mention of the fact or substance of Mr. Letterman's anticipated, actual or potential remarks about Miss Raye, as evidenced by, or about and involving, the March 5 episode.
10.   All scripts, changes or modifications of scripts, rewrites, polishes, touchups, edits or drafts of any anticipated, contemplated, suggested, potential or

163

actual comments or lines of Letterman for the episode at issue of or concerning Ms. Raye or the commercial.

11. All memoranda, notes or correspondence concerning the creation, purpose or objective of the March 5 remarks concerning Martha Raye.

12. Drafts of all proposed scripts or remarks concerning Ms. Raye reviewed by Network Standards, the program attorney, the NBC Legal Department, or the producers or production company's lawyers prior to broadcast.

13. Copies of all editorial, grammatical or factual changes suggested, recommended, considered or made as a result of review by any person described in Paragraph 12 above.

14. Correspondence from or with any person about the Letterman remarks concerning Ms. Raye.

15. All demands for retraction, letters of complaint, inquiries, claims or statements about the truth or falsity of any broadcast remarks authored or contributed to in the last ten years by David Letterman, and all replies or correspondence in connection therewith.

16. Letters or correspondence mentioning, commenting on, or inquiring about the March 5, 1987 remarks concerning Ms. Raye or the facts alleged in the remarks, or Ms. Raye's conduct, and all replies and referrals.

17. The notes of any person pertaining to the origination, facts, circumstances or publication of the remarks, taken or made at conferences, meetings, during editorial or research discussions or meetings, or at any time in the pre-broadcast process.

18. The list of the cast, crew, and observers for the March 5 episode for NBC and the production company.
19. The list of the names of the studio audience, and/or all persons who wrote for or requested tickets for the Letterman Show and who received tickets for or attended the March 5 episode.

Should you fail after due notice to gather, protect, preserve and maintain this evidence to the extent it exists, an instruction as to suppression or destruction of evidence will be requested at trial.

Now, there are some in this great nation of ours who feel that we have become an overly litigious society — our courts clogged with trivial lawsuits, our schools filled with too many attorneys-to-be, our courthouses jammed with rapacious lawyers interested in fees rather than justice, and ambulance chasers preying on both perpetrator and victim.

Am I being overly cynical when I suggest that the pursuit of justice has never been in more noble and inspired hands than those of Martha Raye's legal team? John Jay, Oliver Wendell Holmes and Thurgood Marshall would be proud of their dedication in protecting the reputation and rights of Martha Raye against the nefarious and devious minds of a couple of comedy writers!

Then there are just plain thin of skin. Everyone loves satire, unless, of course, you are being satirized. And those folks could be vocal, especially if the satire was accurate. One of my favorites was telecast at the time that the University of Nevada at Las Vegas was in the midst of a basketball recruiting scandal. *SNL*'s framework was *Paper Chase,* the famous television series about Law School and crusty Professor Kingsley played by John Houseman. Our Kingsley was Academy Award winner Charlton Heston:

OPEN ON: COLLEGE CAMPUS. SUPER 'THE NEW PAPER CHASE'

CUT TO SIGN 'UNIVERSITY OF NEVADA, LAS VEGAS"

CUT TO LECTURE HALL. PHIL, KEVIN, DANA AND VICTORIA ARE STUDENTS.

SUPER: "FIRST DAY OF CLASSES, SPRING TRIMESTER"

DANA (TO VICTORIA)

So what makes you want to take Kingsley's course? You know it's the toughest on campus.

VICTORIA

The toughest course at UNLV? Now that's saying something!

KEVIN

Tell me about it. Every course at UNLV is a killer.

DANA

Well, if you don't like to study…

VICTORIA

I know…don't come to UNLV…

PHIL

Quiet, Kellner, he's starting.

CUT TO PODIUM. CHARLTON HESTON STEPS UP, WEARING CONSERVATIVE SUIT WITH BOW TIE. HE OPENS A BRIEFCASE, PULLS OUT A SHEAF OF NOTES AND SLAPS THEM DOWN. THE ROOM FALLS SILENT.

CHARLTON (ALA JOHN HOUSEMAN)

Good morning. My name is Kingsley, and this is Principles of Blackjack I. Before I begin, permit me to make a few remarks. You come to the University of Nevada Las Vegas with minds full of mush. When you leave you will <u>think like casino operators!</u>

CUT TO STUDENTS LISTENING WITH FEAR

How will you achieve this goal? Through very, very hard work. I will accept no excuse for failure, particularly that most tiresome of all excuses, 'I didn't have the time.' If you have time for pizza with your friends, you have time for blackjack. If you have time to listen to rock and roll music, you have time for blackjack. If you have time for basketball,

CUT TO BLACK STUDENT REACTING

...you have time for blackjack. I trust I have made myself clear. Now then, as this is the introductory lecture of the course, it will be uncharacteristically brief. We begin in earnest on Wednesday, at which time, it goes without saying, you will have completed the assigned reading in Altobelli's (HOLDS BOOK) 'Beating the House the Frank Altobelli Way.' Class dismissed.

Then we saw the students in the library, sweating over "Fundamentals of Casino Greeting" by Joe Louis, trading notes from a Siegfried and Roy lecture and almost cracking under the strain of determining whether a cherry, lemon and gold bar on the slot machines is a winning or losing combination. Back in the classroom, Professor Kingsley is approached by Basketball Coach Jerry Tarkanian, upset because Kingsley had flunked one of his players...

JON (AS TARKANIAN)
Professor, Saturday night we lost to Indiana by four points. If Clarence Briggs had been eligible, we would have beaten the spread.

CHARLTON
Coach Tarkanian, Mr. Briggs failed my exam.

JON
Professor, he correctly identified five of the six chip colors. Isn't that good enough?

CHARLTON
Mr. Tarkanian, five out of six chips might be good enough at other colleges, but while I have anything to say about it, the University of Nevada, Las Vegas will continue to maintain academic standards second to none.

JON
Academic standards. There's that phrase again. It seems like that's all we ever hear about at UNLV. That's what brings the students here. Even my players. Hell, I know they don't care about basketball. To them, basketball is just a ticket to a UNLV education. But sometimes I wonder, what kind of people are we turning out? Oh, sure, when they graduate they can run a craps table, or set up a row of slot machines, or program an air conditioning system. But I can't help thinking — maybe there's a less serious side to life. Is there some small place for athletics at UNLV? I think there is, Professor. What do you think?

CHARLTON (WITH QUIET INTENSITY)
Get out.

***

168

Not content to drive the knife in far enough, Kevin Nealon came out later in the show to say that there'd been a number of phone calls objecting to the sketch and questioning its pertinence... "well, I guess the point we were trying to make, and maybe we didn't'make it very clearly, is that UNLV...isn't really a very good school. Also that the administration standard for basketball players is, well, kind of a joke. We thought that the best way to make our point would be to present this absurd picture of UNLV as a demanding, rigorous school, but I guess many of you misunderstood..."

He went on to say that Las Vegas was a "kind of tawdry and sleazy place..." before asking for no more phone calls.

In this case the satire was ham-handed and hardly close to the satirical genius of Addison and Steele, but not a bad jab at a University then in the news with stories of excesses and shenanigans in its basketball recruitment program. Did we receive letters, you ask? Quite a few, including a gem from the President of the University, Doctor Robert Maxon.

It was no surprise that Doctor Maxon was deeply offended by the attack on his university..."while I realize that the Constitution provides your network with certain protections which permit you to offer satire and criticism, regardless of how unfair, unjustified, or unfunny it might be..." then went on to blast the comments made by Kevin Nealon in the postscript, defending UNLV's curriculum, athletic acceptance standards and, in particular, the city of Las Vegas..."NBC and SNL, virtually overnight, have destroyed years of work by dedicated people who have tried so hard to overcome the false image that your network has perpetuated...the statements mad by Mr. Nealon were tasteless, inappropriate, and inaccurate."

President Maxon did receive a reply from NBC's Vice-President for Press and Public Affairs, although it was hardly the apology that Doctor Maxon may have wanted. It reiterated NBC's oft-stated opinion that SNL had been on the air for many years and that its satire was well-recognized for what it was... "I

169

am sure this letter has not altered your opinion about the merits of what you saw, that is not its purpose. I do want you to know that the skit and the remarks about your university were intended as satire, not as a serious discussion about either the school or Las Vegas itself. We believe most people who saw it would agree."

And need I remind you sports fans that shortly after the telecast, UNLV was placed on athletic probation by the NCAA and that Coach Jerry Tarkanian resigned under pressure brought on by recruiting irregularities. But UNLV's troubles did not end with Tarkanian's ouster. President Maxon was still at the helm when Rollie Massimino was hired to replace Tarkanian. Massimino, the highly-regarded coach at Villanova, did not come cheap. Including a shoe contract, his take-home pay was reported to be $511,000. I'm sure President Maxon was proud of that deal, one of the last under his administration as he left UNLV to become president of a California State College.

But wait, have the sins of UNLV followed him? You bet, witness the following AP wire story from Las Vegas:

> LAS VEGAS: UNLV has no plans to pay basketball coach Rollie Massimino the remainder of nearly $2 million secretly promised in a supplemental contract by former university officials (read Robert Maxon?) UNLV's interim president said Wednesday.
>
> President Kenny Guinn said that since the contract giving Massimino an extra $375,000 above his base salary was never approved by the Board of Regents, the university is not obligated to pay the coach. "If he wants to try and collect the money, he has to ask the people he thinks owes it to him", Guinn said. "It is not my responsibility to try and raise money."
>
> The contract's existence was revealed publicly Wednesday in a copyrighted story in the *Las Vegas Sun*, which said it was secretly set up because Massimino didn't want the full size of his deal made public. With

170

the two other contracts and other perks, Massimino would total nearly $1 million a year under his five year deal.

The extra money was to be paid by a private non-profit organization in addition to the $511,000 he makes a year from UNLV and a shoe contract.

Guinn, who took over as interim president in May from former president Robert Maxon, said Maxon primarily raised the money to pay the extra guarantee, Guinn said Massimino had been paid $300,000 over the past two years in addition to his salary, and is owed $450,000 currently under the contract and another $475,000 next summer.

Guinn said he'd been told by the university system's legal counsel that the university is not obligated to pay the money because it was not approved by the Board of Regents. The money was to have been paid by an organization dubbed 'The Varsity Club,' set up by Maxon and former university legal counsel Brad Brooke to funnel the extra cash to the coach."

Welcome to the world of big-time college athletics, Doctor Maxon. We'll be sure to respect your words criticizing **our** morality. Not!

But, heck, Doctor Maxon isn't alone in his hypocrisy. The satiree never understands that he's brought on the satire by his own actions. In 1980 a Greensboro, North Carolina jury acquitted six Ku Klux Klansmen and American Nazis of charges of murdering five Communist Workers Party members during a "Death to the Klan" rally. Now, how could *SNL* not comment on that probable miscarriage of justice? "Open Season on Commies" was the resultant sketch, set in Greensboro and depicting a group of men milling about, two of them discussing how eager they were to shoot Communists — just like their buddies who were acquitted. One man stood on a box and warned the others to be sure they had their hunting licenses and

171

to hold fire until the hunting season officially began. Just then a shot is fired and the man falls as another cries out, "Jim Boy, you just shot the Governor!"

To no one's surprise, the good people of Greensboro were enraged, and the General Manager of the local NBC affiliate threatened to cancel the show. Now, I have no way of knowing if his heart was really in the complaint, or if he was merely responding to local pressure, but we did apologize abjectly, promising that such a thing would never happen again.

I can assure you, however, that our hearts weren't in the apology.

Censorship feeds the dirty mind more
Than the four-letter word itself would.

— **Dick Cavett**

The networks receive thousands of letters each year from would-be censors deploring current programming and demanding higher standards. Sex and violence, in particular, have spawned a cottage industry whose sole product is a highly organized and well-financed attack on sinful programs. Morality in Media, Accuracy in Media, The National Coalition for Media and CLear-TV all make handsome livings by attacking sex, violence and alleged falsifications in television.

After being flogged by them, it's refreshing to hear from the other side, or is it? One critic of NBC's production of *Mister Roberts* allowed that the network's puritanical code of censorship had robbed the writer of his constitutional right to free speech. In his view, NBC had neutered the script by sanitizing the realistic dialogue of the stage play, the result being humdrum mediocrity. "Why can't network programming be as free to express itself as do the theater, the novel, and now cable? Let the public decide, and if something is objectionable, let them change the channel. After all," he ranted on, "who made the networks the moral arbiters of America?"

Mr. Producer, meet Producer Stephen Bochco (*LA Law, NYPD Blue*, etc.) Bochco once said, "I define the success or failure of what I do by the degree to which I'm able to have an effect on Broadcast Standards. I think that's what makes a show different and better — when you push at the bindings of the medium somewhat. I ruffle an awful lot of feathers because to push at the binding you really have to lean on Broadcast Standards. Doing a series you deal with the standards people more often than the programming department."

Bochco, therefore, saw his mission beyond entertainment as expanding the "bindings" put on his efforts, bindings meaning more than the exclusion of controversial subjects. After all, his programs have dealt with extramarital sex, racism, sexism, police corruption and other dilemmas of law and order. No, to Bochco the bindings represent much more than the inflexibility of the stereotyped censor. What bothers him is any restriction whatsoever on freedom of expression.

But he is between the rock and the hard place. He'd like cops to talk like cops instead of talking in euphemisms. If it were feature pictures, he could use "fuck" and its earthy counterparts in every scene, but there is a significant audience offended by them. As long as the quality control of the network is insisted on, the most offensive words will be deleted. After all, the Supreme Court, the FCC and Congress have backed stations in this area of self-regulation. Language, however, remains a bone of contention, sometimes between Broadcast Standards and its own Programming Department. Over time, as you have undoubtedly noticed, the networks and local stations have accepted more realistic dialogue as the public mood of acceptability changes.

In spite of George S. Kaufman's admonition about satire closing on Saturday night, *Saturday Night Live* has been on the air for twenty-five years, an eternity in television terms and there has been an evolution of acceptability in many areas, reflecting changes in society itself. When Gilda turned to newscaster Jane Curtin and murmured, "Bitch," it was a watershed. Now, while some blasphemous terms such as are still taboo, as are George Carlin's seven words, almost anything else goes. And if you think I'm going to print the seven words, forget it. Actually several are in the preceding pages, but you'll have to find them.

On the other hand, it sometimes works the other way. I inherited a character, Uncle Roy (played by Buck Henry), a perverted baby sitter for two pre-teen girls (Gilda and Laraine.) Uncle Roy loved to put their panties on his head and hide under the glass coffee table to look up their skirts. Yet as we began to understand the prevalence and horror of child abuse and pornography, Uncle Roy thankfully disappeared into television limbo.

As I hope I've made clear, only a trained and sensitive editor can study a script, then juggle the foibles of special interest groups, his own management, advertisers, governmental bodies, an expectant national audience and a vocal creative community without alienating, offending or disappointing one of them. Personalities aside, producers, writers and editors have much in

175

common — a sense of responsibility, skill at negotiation, and a feel for audience expectation. The editor must never fail to respect the fact that the producer, too, is interested in quality control. Before the script hits the editor's desk, the creative team has made innumerable changes and deletions in the interest of balance, propriety and acceptability. One cannot underestimate those who, in many cases are more creative, intelligent and stubborn than oneself. Lorne and Al, I'll never admit to that!

A key word is negotiation. For an editor, the ability to arbitrate, to represent management's position clearly, honestly, tenaciously and, above all, by maintaining a productive human relationship is the secret of survival, especially on *SNL*! The hardest part of the job is to say "No" and make them like it — a paraphrase of Harry Truman's "I learned from history that a leader is a man who has the ability to get other people to do what they don't want to do, and like it."

That is the editor's art, and I think we were pretty good at it. No matter what Al Franken thought, I'd like to think that our supervision and occasional "No way!" helped keep *SNL* on the air all those years. And I'd even like to think that they appreciated it. It was a great ride that I mostly enjoyed. Since no one else wanted the job, it provided me with job security for twelve years, which isn't bad. The cast, writing staff and crew were professional, friendly and sometimes cooperative. But it wouldn't surprise anyone to discover that my pet hate over the twelve years was the music! After all, I grew up with Dorsey, Sinatra, Miller, Goodman et al. While there was an occasional Willie Nelson, Harry Connick, Jr., Anne Murray, the Whiffenpoofs or the cast of *Pirates of Penzance*, it was more often than not Cheap Trick, Captain Beefheart, The Roches, The Kinks, Fear, Simple Minds, or The Cars. At least it impressed my children that I'd met Ric Ocasek, Sheila E or Timbuk 3, whoever they are.

There can be no censorship better
Than one's own conscience.
— **Michelangelo Antonioni**, 1967

A final thought:

In his book, *Where Do You Draw the Line?*, Victor Cline summarizes 36 arguments against censorship, some applying to sex and violence, others to political and religious forms of free expression. Some refer to government censors and some to censorship by Special Interest Groups. Here are some of them:

1. You can't legislate morality. Laws treating morals are inappropriate in a pluralistic society with so many different views at issue.

2. The First Amendment is clear; "Congress shall make no law...abridging the freedom of speech..." Well, that's clear enough. No law! The first function of the First Amendment is to keep debate open. Telling people what they can or cannot read, see or hear is unconstitutional.

3. Where sex is the issue, nobody can define pornography or obscenity. What is dirty to one is merely risque to another.

4. Censoring on the grounds of sex or violence leads to censorship of great works of art or literature. Poor taste is not too great a price to pay for the protection of great art.

5. The real obscenity is not pornography but rather war, poverty, prejudice, racism, sexism and pollution.

6. Censoring sex suggests that sex is bad. Giving pleasure to one another is not bad, but good. That's life. Only those with hang ups are afraid of the healthy depiction of human sexuality.

7. Start censoring books and films and the next step if the censoring of political and economic ideas. The time to resist censorship is in its earliest stages.

8. No proof exists that people, even children, are harmed by erotic imagery. As for crime, the causes

are so diverse that it is impossible to say what influences violent imagery has on would-be law breakers. One school of thought even suggests that seeing erotic or violent images may have a cathartic and therapeutic effect, i.e., pornography keeps the rapist off the street, and violent crime shows act as vicarious outlets for aggressive impulses.

9. Who will censor the censor? Who is really qualified to make judgement? The government, vigilante groups, the PTA, the local vice officer, NBC?

10. Censorship creates a restrictive climate for the artist, smothering creativity, one role of which is to challenge convention and the status quo.

11. The use of erotic or violent imagery is a private, not a public act. The right of adults to purchase such material is protected by a ruling of the Supreme Court.

12. Materials reflecting moral heresy should have the same freedom of expression as those reflecting political heresy. The rights of the best men are secured only as the rights of the vilest and most abhorrent are protected.

13. When you censor something, you give it a "forbidden fruit" aura, thereby creating a sometimes unhealthy interest in it...thus creating a bigger market for it.

14. Censorship never really works. In a democracy, people will get what they want. Prohibition only created a contempt for the law. It did not wipe out drinking.

15. Moral values generated privately by home and church and peers, should be limited privately, not by the public.

16.   If we ignore pornography, it will go away. People will just become bored with it, as happened in Sweden.

17.   Censors are a greater danger to society than what they censor. Moral policemen, fallible in tastes, may become despots. Besides, one never hears censors say that they are hurt by offensive material…it's always the others who are harmed.

In light of all these arguments, then, it would seem that very little freedom of expression could be questioned. Or could it? Actually there are dozens of limitations on one's freedom of expression:

You are not free to shout "Fire!" in a crowded theater.

You are not free to broadcast your beliefs over a loudspeaker at midnight in a residential area.

You are not free to blast from a boombox on a subway train.

You are not free to say libelous things about private citizens.

You are no longer free to advertise cigarettes and liquor on television.

You are not free to plagiarize.

You are not free to publish certain materials considered obscene by a local community.

You are not free to advocate revolution against the American government (even though the American government came into being through violent revolution.)

Free speech, then, is not an <u>absolute</u> right, as Congress has made hundreds of laws that interfere with the rights of expression when those rights are in <u>conflict with other rights.</u> Perhaps, then, we can agree that any limitation of free expression should be the exception, not the rule, and the fact that some may offend does not in itself proscribe such expression.

America's favorite philosopher, Benjamin Franklin, once said, "If all printers were determined not to print anything until they were sure it would offend nobody, there would be very little printed." That is true today, and the Law is willing to let free expression offend, drawing the line at the point of harm.

But the line-drawing is the problem, especially in television. Libertarians argue that morals and ethics are essentially private, and should be left to the home. But that is where the TV is—in the middle of the living room. So, if the home is the place where values should be set, and we don't want the federal government setting our values, then the home must be respected to the extent that we do not invade it with material that parents may find destructive to values that they hold and which they do not wish transmitted to their children.

It's a very fine line, indeed. The courts and legislatures may continue to redefine and find many exceptions to the American commitment to free speech, each representing a trade-off between the perceived harm of unrestrained speech and careful protection of other values.

But noone ever wants to trade off their beliefs. After all, everyone wants television molded to their personal agenda. For example, the religionist complains that "goddam" is blasphemous, the NAACP complains that "nigger" is racist, and the government tells us we may not use George Carlin's seven famous words, words that you will have to find elsewhere.

Aren't these all forms of censorship?

But they are just words, hurtful perhaps, but without the power of ideas which may offend more deeply. Liberals, Conservatives, and middle-of-the-roaders would be horrified at a TV film based on a recent German book suggesting that genocide was not too high a price to pay for the liberation of the German people from economic servitude and political anarchy. No responsible network would touch that with the proverbial

181

ten-foot pole, and rightly so. No one complains about such censorship.

On the other hand, millions of conservative Americans feel that the airwaves are permeated with the endorsement of promiscuity and the condonation of recreational and pre-marital sexual behavior striking at the heart of stable, Judeo-Christian family life.

Rhetorically, why is the censorship of fascism as an idea, permissible? And why is the censorship of fornication as an idea, not permissible?

There's that line again.

So, perhaps what we're really saying is that it's not so much a matter of being for or against censorship <u>on television</u> as it is a matter of what kind of censorship we want. Hence we must hammer out the solution on the middle ground—from a moderate position. No matter how loud Steven Bochco screams that "That's the way people talk!" — it is true that only some people talk that way, and the majority of the viewing public does not wish to have "fuck," "shit," and "cocksucker" beamed into their living rooms. To hear such language, just go into any motion picture theater and buy a ticket.

Values and liberty must be upheld, so there must be compromise, powered by considerations of consequence, and the feelings and attitudes of others. So there stands our editor, our Horatius in the middle of the bridge, making moral and taste judgements, all the while withstanding whatever criticism they might bring.

Does TV pander? Perhaps, but I prefer to think TV <u>leans</u> to the side of restraint, properly so because TV is, essentially, a guest—not just in your home, but in every home in the nation. Isn't such moderation the best path? Surely there's a middle ground in a pluralistic society—a ground between <u>expression</u> and <u>license.</u>

In television it's called Broadcast Standards.

My career ended when NBC's new owners—none other than my old pals at General Electric — decided that the solid citizens of America could do without much Standards protection. GE "downsized" Broadcast Standards in 1988 from a staff of 40 to 10. One of those downsized was Ralph Daniels, an executive of the old school who had deep-rooted, genuine moral standards. Responsibility for what was left of his department was turned over to executives of the new school who have, as far as I can see, few moral standards of any kind.

GE's theory was that Standards' responsibilities could easily be taken over by the programming executives assigned to each show, sort of like inmates running the asylum. What they hadn't considered was that the program executives all wanted to eventually go to work for the very producers the network would have them censor. It was a system bound to fail, and it did, immediately. In rapid succession, NBC's programmer/censors gave the okay to a gruesome Geraldo Rivera Special on Satan worshippers and a lurid miniseries called *Favorite Son*. The former featured descriptions of babies skinned alive, the latter contained scenes of bondage and of a dog lapping at a pool of blood from a corpse. An uproar ensued, and GE had no choice but to put some censors back on the job. I hung on for awhile but eventually I was downsized, too. By that time the atmosphere at NBC was so depressing I was just as happy to be gone.

I paid my last visit to *SNL* on the night of December 15, 1990, saying goodbye to my old friends on the show and officially turning it over to the censor who was replacing me. (Yes, there's still a censor on *Saturday Night Live*. Always was. Even GE isn't stupid enough to downsize that far.) I was standing backstage during rehearsal when Lorne Michaels mentioned that they were planning some sort of acknowledgement of my retirement on Weekend Update, would I mind? Touched, I said of course not. Not long after that somebody brought me Dennis Miller's script…"Tonight we want to bid a fond adieu to William Clotworthy, the gentleman who has been our network censor for the past twelve years. Yes, he's a good guy. So long, Bill, we're going to miss you, you lovable old jackoff."

I laughed when I read it, but I squirmed a little, too. The language was a little raw, even by *SNL*'s standards. Definitely questionable. Should it get on unedited? "It's your call, Bill!" a few people from the show shouted. "It's your last call — you gotta make it."

I knew I was being set up here: How could I possibly edit a farewell message to myself? My replacement probably saw it was a set up, too, but he graciously (or cowardly) deferred the decision to me. I didn't hesitate a second. Hell yes, it got on! What did I care if Reverend Wildmon started a new campaign against NBC on Monday morning?

It was my call, but it wouldn't be my problem.

Hollywood Daze

Nobody asked me, but it's my book so I can write about anything I want, right? Now, the *SNL* stuff is all over, so if you want to stop, it's your decision. However I'm going to tell some additional stories about my 20 years as an advertising executive, program supervisor and commercial producer in LaLa Land.

In December 1952, the American Tobacco Company bought a traveling radio show called "The American Way," starring the bandleader Horace Heidt. Horace was well-known for a previous program "Youth Opportunity," a glorified amateur show featuring young performers. "The American Way" was the same idea, in which he would take his band and a troupe of youthful performers on a series of one-night stands under the aegis of Lucky Strike cigarettes. Try and get away with that appeal today! In any event, I was assigned to accompany this group as the BBDO representative, incidentally producing a weekly radio show. Whose idea was this? This was just at the time when TV was taking over America, and we bought a radio show!

In any event, after six months traversing all 48 states, we ended up in Hollywood. Since I was single and the show was collapsing, I was asked to transfer to BBDO's Hollywood office. And there I stayed for the next 22 years! Right in the Taft Building at the corner of Hollywood and Vine, at that time one of America's most famous intersections.

I thought this was pretty glamorous stuff until one day I was standing on the corner waiting for the light to change and sensed I was being watched. I looked down at a car full of tourists peering up at me as if I were a major star. Did I feel shattered when the woman in the front seat said, with sneering disappointment, "Oh, keep driving, Lester. He's nobody!"

Another time there was a media advertising contest in Los Angeles won by the BBDO office, the first prize being an hour of telephone switchboard time donated by Lily Tomlin as her famous character from *Laugh-In*, Ernestine the Telephone

Operator. Lily showed up bright and early one morning, but didn't know how to run the console, so she just answered calls in that whining, obnoxious voice that cut through like a knife. Just my luck, the very first call was for me, and Lily's end of the conversation went something like this:

"Mister who? Mister Flotworther? Mr. Plotenfelter? Oh, Clotworthy! What a silly name! I'm sorry, sir, but there's no one here by that name. Call later. I'm just going to hang up now, it's time for my coffee break."

The "sir" turned out to be BBDO's creative director, calling from New York. He was a man not known for an understanding heart nor sense of humor. He was not amused.

Hollywood personalities love causes; wrapping themselves in cloaks of respectability, although some carry their beliefs to extremes. One time we were looking for a beautiful young actress to appear in a glamorous bathtub while extolling the virtues of Dove Soap, a Lever Brothers product known for its softening ingredients. Our choice was Tyrone Power's lovely daughter, Taryn. The deal was set and a shooting date scheduled. There was no costume call since she was presumably working in the nude. Well, in a bikini under suds.

At literally the last moment, however, she refused to do the commercial! No, she wasn't intimidated by the scene, it turned out she was an animal rights activist who had actually researched the product; to discover to her horror that Dove's secret softening ingredient was lanolin, a sheep by-product. That no-no caused her to reject participation as a matter of principle, even giving up an excellent payday.

Oh, I caught hell for that one, especially as our last-minute substitute, Jennifer O'Neill, jacked up her price, knowing we were in a bind. She wasn't too thrilled with doing a bathtub scene, but overcame her nervousness with frequent glasses of rose wine.

Hollywood personalities have always been politically active, although few have aspired to office. George Murphy served a term as United States Senator, Fred Grandy left a glamorous job as purser on *The Love Boat* to become a congressman, and Ronald Reagan switched from the make-believe world of Hollywood to the fantasy world of Sacramento and Washington, DC. During each presidential election, a number of votes are written in for Mickey Mouse or Fred Flintstone but, regretfully, Hollywood's other perennial candidate has never succeeded in gaining higher office. That would be comedian Pat Paulsen, whose quadrennial candidacy garnered few votes. I once attended a fund-raiser for Pat. In line with his less-than-serious campaigning, dinner at the Ontra Cafeteria in Beverly Hills cost each contributor only 89 cents (tax-deductible) that included red jug wine and all the spaghetti once could eat! It was, as you can imagine, an entertaining affair with Carl Reiner as emcee and most of the top comedians on hand. It was announced that Pat's political war chest had been increased by $1.37, after expenses.

I produced and directed a tremendous number of commercials, some of which stand out because of their sheer nuttiness. Once we produced a campaign for Standard Oil of California called "Wiki-Wiki Dollars," a gimmicky rebate and giveaway offer using silly-looking Polynesian scrip. The commercials featured a hula dancer (the enchanting Irene Tsu) on top of a gas pump, gyrating away to the beat of jungle drums and the vocal incantation of "Wiki-Wiki, Wiki-Wiki...," well, surely you get the idea. The composer of this epic was not a Hawaiian but a Greek-American named George Roumanis, who attended the pre-production meeting in San Francisco where he was asked by the client to perform the jingle. George looked around, then picked up his briefcase as a drum and bongoed the beat as he chanted the inspired lyrics.

At the final recording session a few weeks later, George shipped in a large collection of Polynesian and jungle gourds and drums so that we'd get the authentic sound. The drummer, Irv Cottler (Sinatra's drummer!) banged away on all of them, but the client just didn't hear what he thought was right. "George, what was the sound I heard in San Francisco? That was perfect!"

You've guessed it. Wiki-Wiki Dollars went on the air with what was undoubtedly the only sound track utilizing a musical briefcase!

I loved musical commercials as the finest studio musicians were involved. Irv Cottler, Jack Sperling, Manny Klein, Ziggy Elman, Paul Smith, Barney Kessel, Herb Ellis and dozens of others were delighted to pick up nice residual payments by playing in jingles for Lucky Lager, Gallo wine or Dodge cars. And anonymously.

George Roumanis and I were involved with a musical spot for the San Francisco Dodge Dealers, a western ditty called "The Dodge Boys." How original. We decided to corn it up with a country singing voice, so George tapped the five-string guitar player in the band — a young man newly-arrived in Hollywood — to do the honors. Oh, how I wish I'd saved the tape of the singing debut of Glen Campbell!

The jingle business was fascinating and particularly rewarding because I worked with such terrific musicians. Paul Weston did a job for Armstrong, John Scott Trotter was Bing Crosby's musical conductor, Nelson Riddle wrote and conducted commercials for Dodge and I worked with the Randy Van Horne Singers, Jud Conlon and his Rhythmaires, Perry Botkin, Jr., and Bobby Troup. Western Airlines once ran a campaign featuring flights to Mexico and I produced authentic sounds with famous guitarist Laurindo Almeido and some less than authentic with Julius Wechter and the Baja Marimba Band!

I even produced a singing commercial with the late Henry Mancini, the Academy Award composer ("Moon River" and others). No, Hank didn't write, conduct or arrange. He sang! Schaefer Beer, a New York-based product, was sponsoring a "Guess the Singer" contest in which the performer sang the Schaefer jingle, and I was asked to find someone in Hollywood, not known as a singer, and overdub their voice on an existing musical track. Hank was an old acquaintance from his days as a staff arranger at Universal and I imposed on that old friendship. He was willing, so swearing our engineer to absolute secrecy, I recorded Henry Mancini's singing debut, a debut that was also his finale. What a talent. Composing and conducting, that is.

Nelson Riddle was in my office one day when he glanced at his watch, remarking that he had to leave to meet Nat Cole at the Brown Derby and would I like to join them for a drink? Would I? Nelson was concerned, for Cole was uncomfortable waiting by himself in a "white" establishment. This was the early 50s, he had his own national television program, was one of the most popular singers of his day, lived and worked within a liberal industry and community — but was still "uncomfortable." Our meeting was social but I found him a man of great charm and dignity. Unfortunately he was a heavy smoker, a great talent taken by lung cancer far too early

Through Nelson I met his agent, Carlos Gastel, who in turn introduced me to his associate, Jack Leonard. Jack Leonard, big band vocalist with Tommy Dorsey ("Marie") and predecessor of Frank Sinatra with the Dorsey band! A terrific talent, a nice man, and a warm memory from my youth. Then there was the Bob Crosby Show at CBS that featured The Modernaires and The Bobcats. I could hardly wait to cover that show each day, a one-hour, five days a week musical variety show. Johnny Carson had a daytime show and I also covered an NBC strip that starred guitarist Roy Clark and lovely Molly Bee, sort of an early day Barbara Mandrell.

I don't know that I actually "discovered" anyone, but impressionist Rich Little's first job in Hollywood was as "Daring Dan Waverly" in commercials for Lucky Lager beer. Lucky also gave a break to a young and talented black singer named Lou Rawls (He was paid $100 for a demo, and was happy to get it!) and an ambitious model, Mary Tyler Moore, appeared as an extra in an early commercial for a perfume account.

One time a hotshot creative guy from our San Francisco office came down to shoot a test spot for Gallo. He had a bright concept sure to please everyone—the idea based on "the kiss of the grapes" — featuring a deeply decolleted actress practically humping the lens, pursing her lips and murmuring, "Kiss me, squeeze me" as she smooched the camera. A few hours of observing that and we all ran home to jump the bones of our wives but, contrary to our hopes, BBDO's New York Plans Board took one look and we could hear their shout across the country, "Not from stuffy old BBDO!"

And while "Kiss me, squeeze me" may have set back a creative career, it certainly didn't hurt the actress, Raquel Welch.

Commercials were a lot of fun, and I not only produced hundreds on both television and radio, but assisted other producers with casting. Casting is the most important phase of commercial production as the message is so short and the actors must convey instant persona. I'm always amused when I watch television and spot someone who'd been in the office on a casting call, especially if we'd rejected them. These include Cheryl Ladd (nee Stoppelmoor), Tom Selleck, Don Johnson, Annette Funicello, Maureen Reagan and many others.

Without question my most embarrassing casting job was for Right Guard Ladies Deodorant, calling for a beautiful young lady to work with a lion. I believe the message had to do with the strength of the deodorant and the delight of femininity, but don't ask for too much logic, this was a commercial. However, it seems that male wild animals are sensitive to human menstruation so that, as part of the casting interview, I had to ask each applicant her current mentrual schedule!

And stage mothers! Yes, they can be as determined as they're portrayed. I passed through a crowd of candidates one day and heard a mother hiss to her 12 year-old, "Remember, you're seven!"

Commercials were often lucrative for performers, but not always easy. We were involved with a show at Ziv called "Favorite Story" hosted by the dapper Adolphe Menjou. The show was syndicated throughout the country and sponsored by about ten different beers in their respective marketing areas. Menjou sat in a library set with a bottle of beer and a glass, smiled into the camera, introed the program, then poured a foaming glass of the product with loving care. When he'd finished, a stagehand would bring in a fresh glass and a different beer and Menjou would repeat the same spiel. It's a damned good thing he didn't have to drink each one!

I did a wonderful series of commercials for Northwestern Bell Telephone, featuring personalities and athletes who'd grown up in Minnesota, the Dakotas, Iowa or Nebraska, talking about their memories and the importance of touching their roots by calling home (by phone.) That gave me the opportunity to meet Pitchers Bob Gibson and Bob Feller, Ann Sothern, Myron Floren and, best of all, Harriet Nelson. Naturally Ozzie became involved and it turned out that he and I came from adjoining towns in New Jersey and had mutual friends. Harriet performed in the commercial but Ozzie handled the paperwork that included what I thought was a rather ordinary standard contract for her service, but Ozzie spotted humor in it, as follows:

"...as to the contract itself, it is a most unusual document. It's refreshing in these days of rush, rush, rush where most people only devote a brief paragraph to such an authorization, that your people had the diligence and persistence to devote two full pages to the matter.

I also liked the rich literary style—sort of a combination of Spiro Agnew and early Muhammad Ali — for instance I not only 'consent,' I 'irrevocably consent. The consideration I receive is 'full and adequate' and is received by 'virtue' (a word we hear so seldom in these days of sexual freedom) of the 'first' such use...not the second or third but the very first.

My favorite paragraph, however, is the one where I indemnify 'at all times' not only the sponsor and the agency but also their 'servants.'

Any firm that is this solicitous about their footmen, butlers, chambermaids etc., can't be all bad."

BBDO's legal department was not amused.

Another of the Northwestern Bell spots starred Edgar Bergen, who hailed from Minnesota. Following a pre-production meeting at his office on Sunset Boulevard, he invited a few of us to his home for cocktails. We drove to Beverly Hills to be greeted by a 15 year-old vision of loveliness, Candice Bergen, even then charming and sophisticated. We were also introduced to Charlie McCarthy, lying in state in a special box in Edgar's den. And why not? Edgar's success and worldly goods were due to his relationship with Charlie.

Charlie's shrine reminded me of Harpo Marx' home where a dramatically-lit niche housed his favorite harp.

I was a child of radio and got particular pleasure from associating with the old-time radio people, whether Edgar Bergen or announcers Andre Baruch, Ken Carpenter, Harry Von Zell or Mr. First Nighter, Olan Soule. Incidentally, you'll be delighted to know that Andre Baruch's given name is Andre Bernard Jean Jacques Rousseau Octavius le Troiseme Baruch de la Pardo, but that Don Pardo's is not. The answer to another trivia question, incidentally, is that Wolfman Jack's real name is Bob Smith. I was personally close to Suspense's Larry Thor and Groucho's sidekick, George Fenneman. Another pal, and he didn't have many, was Jack Benny's stooge, Frank (Weeeellll!) Nelson, not because he wasn't a nice guy, but because he was an active and outspoken union activist. And what can you say about lovable Mel Blanc except that there has never been a more unusual talent — nor a nicer man.

The voice specialists, as a group, were talented, close-knit, and fun. Don Messick, Shep Mencken, Daws Butler, June Foray, Stan Freberg, Joan Gerber and all of the other unsung heroes of animation were marvelous and cooperative people. Bugs Bunny, Elmer Fudd, Yogi Bear, Rocky and Bullwinkle, the Jetsons and many others became alive through the talents of those folks.

Another privilege of working in Hollywood was my long association with major personalities — Groucho Marx, Bing Crosby and Jack Benny. Ironically they passed away within months of one another, inspiring me to write the following piece for the BBDO Newsletter:

I Remember Bing, Jack andGroucho

Three superstars passed away recently. Jack Benny. Groucho. Bing.

Interestingly, all were on radio for BBDO and made their television program debuts for BBDO clients. I had the singular honor of representing BBDO on those shows and what a thrill it was to be associated with three of the greatest entertainers of our time.

Jack Benny debuted on television for Lucky Strike cigarettes in late 1952, live from New York on CBS. His entire cast and staff came to New York from Hollywood and preparations for that first show were a shambles with Don Wilson and Mary Livingstone down with the flu, and other countless problems and pressures that only live television could cause.

I remember that during the dinner break between dress rehearsal and airtime I returned to the studio to check on the commercial set (remember Dorothy Collins in the Lucky Strike bullseye?), where I found Jack Benny wandering alone on the deserted stage, looking at and touching the cameras and other electronic gear.

I thought he looked nervous…his wife and cast members were ill, he was entering a new era of show business, he had personal and professional problems and much to lose…when he realized I was standing there, he swept his arm around the studio and said, "Isn't this wonderful? Isn't this exciting?"

That's how I'll remember Jack. The consummate professional. No matter how bleak the outlook, no matter how important the stakes, he was looking forward to a new professional challenge with wonder, awe and confidence.

Groucho Marx made his television debut for DeSoto-Plymouth in 1950 on NBC. Groucho was a closet intellectual. Without much formal education he was thoughtful, erudite and included great literary figures among his intimates. He was much more comfortable with writers than other performers.

He was basically shy and was a warm man. In late 1955 he found out my wife had just given birth and subjected me to a masterful "first-time father" ribbing during a program warm up. But after the show he made a point to congratulate me privately and to invite me and my wife to dinner, which we gratefully accepted and enjoyed.

Bing Crosby had a network radio program for General Electric in 1953 that led to his TV debut for GE in January 1954, one of the first "specials." Bing was an innovator in the mechanical/electronic age and he learned to use the medium to enhance his natural style. As an early investor in AMPEX, he experimented with quarter-inch audio tape in the 40s, which was the forerunner of the multi-track audiotape and advanced color videotape that we use today. Actually. after Bing left the Paul Whiteman band in 1934, he performed in a professional vacuum, that is, motion pictures and the recording studio. Live audiences attended his network radio show, but when he could record and edit shows on tape and then add audience effects, he produced even those in the privacy of the studio.

Our GE radio show was recorded on Sunday morning (right after Bing attended mass) in a huge theater, before an audience consisting of me and Bing's publicity man! From that time on, he made rare public appearances until recently when he concertized with his new family. Naturally his TV debut for us was also on film. No live performance for him.

And talk about erudition. Bing was a very bright and genuinely witty man with a great vocabulary and a photographic mind. We asked him to do a public service message one time. He glanced at it, we rolled camera, and he delivered the message verbatim, within time, with no retakes.

In these days of split sponsorship and scatter buying, it is doubtful we'll see very much of the long and productive agency/client/artists relationships again. Of course, great new stars will come along to replace those we've lost, but I know that all of us will always remember with great fondness Jack Benny...Groucho...and Bing.

Bing's radio show featured many musical guests such as Frank Sinatra, Louis Armstrong and Ella Fitzgerald who was the subject of the finest professional compliment I've ever witnessed. It was the Christmas show (recorded in September, as I recall) and Bing asked Ella to join him in singing "White Christmas." Her mouth fell open and she mumbled something like, "Oh, that's your song, Mr. Bing...I just couldn't..." But he insisted and away they went. It was the first time anyone had sung the song with Bing since the movie in which it was introduced. Remember, at the climax of "Holiday Inn," Marjorie Reynolds, on the set of a movie, pining for Jim Hardy (Bing), sings the first chorus before noticing Bing's pipe on the piano, realizes he is on the set and that she loves him, not that nasty character played by Fred Astaire, and...oh, it was so romantic!

Several years later Bing did a little fifteen minute radio show with Rosemary Clooney and the Buddy Cole trio, again for GE. I often wonder if those tapes are gathering dust in the vaults at CBS-Radio, for they should be reissued as they were fabulous entertainment — two great singing stars at the peak of their talent.

GE finally persuaded Bing to enter the TV arena with a sixty minute special at Christmas time. It featured guest spots by Jack

Benny and a young dancer named Sheree North, whose most obvious talent was as the current girlfriend of Bing's head writer, Bill Morrow. Since this was a very important program, BBDO sent a top New York executive to supervise, not trusting their young and inexperienced Hollywood producer, me. The executive was Arthur Pryor, a wonderful and gregarious guy, son of the famous American bandleader.

Unfortunately, Arthur was a middle-aged letch who couldn't keep his eyes off Miss North in her modest dancing costume, its fringe bouncing whenever she did. In today's moral climate we would find the ensuing flap to be laughable, but when the film was sent back to GE, the proverbial souffle hit the fan and poor Arthur found himself in deep doodoo for allowing such lascivious behavior on a General Electric program. He wasn't fired, but he didn't get any more fun trips to California either. I just thanked the good Lord that Arthur, and not yours truly, had been the responsible agency executive on hand, because you know I was staring at Sheree North right along with Arthur.

One of the first stars I met in Hollywood was, of all people, Richard Burton, who was making his Hollywood debut in *Prince of Players*, the story of John Wilkes Booth. He apparently was conned by his publicist to participate in a "Guess Whose Eyes?" contest sponsored by my client, DeSoto. In addition to a new car, the winner got to meet the actor to whom the eyes belonged— and guess who accompanied the winners to Paramount to meet this young, unknown and utterly charming personality no one had heard of at that time. Oh, why didn't I have the foresight to get autographs or pictures of these struggling folks?

I was involved with many star-filled commercials during my tenure with the agency. I made the deal with Rex Harrison when he lowered himself to appear in *My Fair Lady* spots for Dodge, although a $250,000 fee and unlimited vodka may have been instrumental. When his contract ran out he was replaced by the charming continental dreamboat, Louis Jourdan.

Florence Henderson for Wesson Oil, William Shatner for Promise Margarine, Monty Hall for Rexall, Paul Ford, Fred

Gwynne and Imogene Coca as Ceiling Doctors for Armstrong and Eddie Albert for Pillsbury were among my favorites. There were flops, of course. One time the "mad genius" creative director had a real brainstorm (we called it a nightmare.) He had created the "Have it Your Way" campaign for Burger King and took a proprietary interest in it, so when Frank Sinatra had a major hit with "My Way" the mad genius dreamed of a commercial in which Sinatra would sing "My Way" as a paean to the hamburger, having it "his way." With mustard and onions, hold the mayo.

No matter how absurd the idea or inadequate the compensation, an offer must be made to the artist's agent. He, in turn, has a fiduciary responsibility to present it to the artist. And we were prepared to offer a lot more than cash — Burger King stock, distributor participation, etc. Sinatra did not have an agent per se, as all deals were handled by his personal attorney, Mickey Rudin, whom I'd met and who actually returned my call. After his laughter subsided and he had asked the inevitable, "Why in hell would Mr. Sinatra do such a dumbass thing?" he asked for storyboards and presumably went through the motions of discussing the offer with Sinatra who, predictably, rejected it. The creative genius couldn't believe that anyone would reject his brilliant idea. Filled with his own importance, he was infuriated, not with Sinatra, but with me for blowing the deal! I know that our musical director was spared the indignity of having to tell him that the composer of "My Way," Paul Anka, was, at the same time, refusing to sell the commercial rights as he was pissed off at Sinatra's success with the song. Talk about ill-fated projects.

Have you seen a restaurant or crowd scene in a movie with people in the background talking to one another, and wonder what they were saying? Well, here's the news you've been waiting for. The crowd murmur is everyone going "Wawasasafafa," pronounced "wah-wah-sah-sah-fah-fah." Listen carefully the next time.

In over twenty years of working in Hollywood, that is surely one of the more interesting and useful bits of information taught by Danny Kaye. The Danny Kaye Show was sponsored by our client, Armstrong, and lasted a couple of years but should have gone on forever. The writing was literate and funny, the music by Paul Weston and the secondary players, Joyce Van Patten and Harvey Korman, were brilliant as were the guest stars. He even had Kate Smith! The show, however, was never a blockbuster in the ratings. Perhaps it was the time period or even Danny. Maybe he didn't come across on the small screen that tends to emphasize superficiality and lack of genuine feeling. Danny was not the warm and sincere person he was purported to be, and I never thought he really liked kids! And his Chinese cooking wasn't so hot, either.

Speaking of food, *Gidget* caused a client problem in one episode that featured a food fight in the school cafeteria. The kids weren't throwing soup at each other, but client Campbell Soup was sensitive to any disrespect to food, and the offending scene was deleted. Shades of GE and the broken radio! Clients did seem to overreact at times, protective of their images, but service was the name of the advertising game, which led to frequent silliness. Remember the Sheraton commercials featuring gorgeous model Barbara Rucker selling 1-800-355-8585 from glamour spots around the world? I will now tell you that she never would have gotten the job without my involvement. We had to make sure that she could swim, for a commercial set on the beach in Bali, so I drove to her condo at the marina, observed this sexy creature swim a lap or two, then drove back to report, "She can swim."

The longest trip to the land of advertising stupidity was a drive to Ensenada, Mexico. Our client, DuPont, was sponsoring a series of Specials featuring writer George Plimpton participating in various unusual events — as a trapeze artist in a circus, an extra in a John Wayne western, standup comic in Las Vegas, in this case co-driver with Parnelli Jones in the Baja California over-the-road race. The Jones-Plimpton car was

198

supposed to be adorned with a DuPont logo, but it wasn't ready in time before the car shipped to Mexico. Therefore I was dispatched to drive from LA to Ensenada carrying the logo to George and Parnelli. The trip didn't compare to carrying the serum to Nome, nor the message to Garcia, but off I went in my trusty Buick, thankfully arriving in time to affix the decal before the race began. When the show aired, however, the car was bouncing around so much that it was almost impossible to see the logo!

The hideaway of the stars was Palm Springs, which I first visited in 1952 after a harrowing drive across the mountains from San Diego in a blinding snowstorm. The driver was Charlie Russhon, director of *Meet The Champ* and, as I recall, we just wanted to get away from the disaster of losing Red Mountain and our program. I'll never forget waking the next morning to see the magnificent setting, the bright sunshine and the imposing mountains we'd been stupid enough to traverse the night before. I've been in love with Palm Springs ever since, although I didn't have the brains (nor the wherewithal) to invest in a town that at the time had but two golf courses, one deli, a handful of hotels, an unlimited future — and no traffic!

Palm Springs, of course, can be oppressive in the summer. I shot a commercial at a gas station one Memorial Day weekend when the thermometer read 125 degrees, and the concrete surrounding our hotel pool was too hot to walk on. With sandals. And there were sandstorms. I drove to the Springs to record a radio spot with Eddie Cantor (Is there another producer living who's worked with Eddie Cantor?) and on the way home I got caught in a blinding storm that not only forced sand into the car, but pitted the windshield so badly it had to be replaced.

The tremendous growth of Palm Springs was not necessarily due to the movement to the desert of Hollywood stars, but to the age of air conditioning and the availability of water for swimming pools and golf courses. Then the stars came, along with major hotels, condominiums, the Aerial tramway, shopping centers, New York-style delicatessens — and so much congestion that a drive down Palm Canyon Drive is an adventure, and a darned slow one at that.

For one 26-week period I drove to Palm Springs from the San Fernando Valley every single weekend for the production of a little barter show called *Visual Girl*, also sponsored by DuPont. We shot this gem at a local station on Sunday morning when normal people might be expected to be at church, or on the golf course. It was not the sort of schedule designed to please the family back home, especially a jealous wife who didn't appreciate any involvement with the cast of *Visual Girl* — six nubile teenaged girls. She was particularly upset when she saw a commercial for Lycra, the selling point of which was that Lycra did not cause "panty line" and proved it with tight closeups of the rear end of a pubescent teeny bopper as she swung her fanny up onto a horse or bent over to pick flowers. Oh, why do they send good family men on shoots like that?

General Electric Theatre was cancelled after a long and successful run, victimized by the runaway success of its competition, *Bonanza*. As a last gasp, GE experimented with live-on-tape productions from CBS TV City, but nothing worked. One show, however, stands out. It was "Mr. O"Malley," starring the incomparable Bert Lahr as the fantasy companion of a lonely little boy. It was a difficult part for a child, but Ethel Winant, CBS's brilliant casting director, discovered a delightful kid who filled the screen with personality, talent and presence. Somehow we all knew he was destined for a successful acting career, but no one could have predicted the directing and production skills of five year-old Ron Howard.

It's possible, of course, that *GE Theatre* took a dive when they cast Tony Curtis to play young David in *The Stone*, the story of David and Goliath. Tony tried hard, but ears were jarred all over the nation when David prayed for strength, "Oh, Lawd, Lawd, give me the strength!" Somehow his Brooklyn accent seemed out of place in the Sinai.

During the last season of *GE Theatre*, someone came up with a promotional gimmick in the form of a 30-minute radio interview between Ronald Reagan and that week's star. The two did not meet, however. Ronnie's questions and the star's answers were recorded separately, then pieced together. Engineer Dave Gold and I recorded these epics in dressing rooms, homes, restaurants, offices, even while sipping drinks at Steve Allen's pool. We recorded Lorne Greene on the set of *Bonanza* and Rod Steiger on the set when he was portraying Joseph Stalin. For cuing purposes, I played Ronnie and it was disconcerting, to say the least, to have Joseph Stalin glaring at you when you asked innocuous questions such as, "Did you enjoy working with your wife, Claire Bloom?"

GE was reluctant to lose its valuable time period, so one more attempt was made with *GE True*, a dramatic program that featured stories from the pages of *True Magazine*. The Creator/Executive Producer was the legendary Jack Webb, the creator/star/producer/director/resident genius of *Dragnet*. Jack had the reputation of stubbornness mixed with a healthy dose of ego and temper. Believe me, I entered our relationship with some trepidation, but the fears were unfounded. Jack was no pussycat, definitely stubborn and very opinionated. On the other hand, he was totally honest — a committed producer who delivered on his promise to "put the money on the screen." He produced excellent programs that were not, more's the pity, any more successful in competing with *Bonanza* than was *General Electric Theatre*.

GE True was produced at Warner Brothers, owned by one of the last of the great motion picture pioneers, Jack Warner. Jack Webb had a warm relationship with Warner and whenever we were blessed with a visit from the New York brass we'd be treated to a Jack Warner-hosted lunch in his private dining room. Warner was close to eighty, tended to ramble a bit, and considered himself a comedian and raconteur. The lunch was invariably a monologue in which he told a string of bum jokes and personal philosophy, even his secret of longevity: "I pee a lot." Strange, I can't find that bit of wisdom in *Bartlett's Quotations.*

Meeting one's heroes can be disappointing. We bought a show, *Annie Oakley,* produced by cowboy actor legend Gene Autry. At a pre-noon production meeting he was already in the bag. Lee Marvin starred in *M Squad*, mostly shot in a bar across from Universal Studios since that's where he was most of the time. Host Bob Crosby spent his after-show career at the bar at Rand's Roundup. Lovable character actor Don Ameche and comedian Billy DeWolfe proved not so lovable, and composer-singer Hoagy Carmichael could have been the third lead in *Grumpy Old Men.*

There were two stars who totally intimidated me. One was Fred Astaire, my hero of heroes, the greatest entertainer of my lifetime. He appeared on *GE Theatre* a time or two, and I couldn't bring myself to approach him. The other was Gracie Allen. One of our BBDO clients, BF Goodrich Tires, sponsored the *Burns and Allen Show* for many years. Our representative on the show, Larry Algeo, was well aware of my admiration of Gracie, the funniest woman on the face of the earth. Gracie dined with co-star Bea Benadaret at the Brown Derby each week before the filming session and Larry offered to introduce me to Gracie many times. Somehow I never got up the nerve to walk fifty feet down Vine Street to the restaurant, afraid that a meeting would forever shatter an image so important to me.

I have regretted not meeting Lucille Ball, however, and had a real chance. I'd been widowed, and remarried, tying the knot with a widow with four children. Since I had three children and we subsequently had one of our own, we lived a true life, albeit smaller, version of Lucy's film *Yours, Mine, and Ours*, based on the life of the Beardsley family who had a combination of fifteen! Lucy's publicist was a friend who arranged for our family to see the movie together and I wrote Lucy a note of thanks. She replied with a gracious invitation to attend the taping of her show, but for whatever reason we never took her up on it. I suspect my wife was afraid we'd be pointed out and she didn't want people to know she was the mother of eight! Lord knows she didn't look it.

As an old hambone I didn't mind such attention, although it is a bizarre experience to see oneself portrayed on the screen. I am not referring to the gentle spoof on *Saturday Night Live*. During my tenure with *GE Theatre*, I was involved with a dramatic personal situation that I developed into a story that I sold to the program. When my first wife was pregnant with our third child, a serious, life-threatening heart condition was diagnosed as mitral insufficiency, thus beginning a 3-month adventure prompted by the obstetrician's opinion that a therapeutic abortion need be performed; that a continued pregnancy would jeopardize Joyce's life. Hence we were face to face with ethical, religious, legal and medical decisions that had to be made immediately.

In California, a therapeutic abortion could not be performed without three separate medical opinions, one of which was already known. A visit to a leading cardiologist led to an opinion that the baby could be carried safely. Then it was to another cardiologist named Goodman, a man we did not know, but whose examination resulted in another positive opinion. As you can imagine, the last months of the pregnancy were nerve-wracking, but a fine daughter was delivered without complication. The story was telecast as *GE Theatre's* Easter program in 1962 with Geraldine Brooks as my wife and Earl Holliman playing me. Earl's a good actor, although I had hoped for John Wayne, who I was told, was unavailable.

After twelve years in the hot seat of *Saturday Night Live*, I faced the dreaded year of decision, the Big 65! What to do in retirement if one wished to remain active. What kind of work does censorship prepare one for anyway? I took a stab at magazine writing with some success but then some particularly nasty mud-slinging during a political campaign inspired an article on the history of presidential campaign insults, an idea that did not sell. The research, however, got me into the library where I began to view presidents on a slightly higher level, resulting in a book, *Homes and Libraries of the Presidents*, an interpretive guidebook to 88 presidential homes, libraries and museums concentrating on those places open to public visitation, ranging from the colonial masterpieces of Mount Vernon and Monticello to the rude cabin birthplace of Abraham Lincoln and the small-town homes of Ronald Reagan and William McKinley.

As a companion piece, I completed *Presidential Sites*, a monumental directory of every extant place in America associated with presidents — birthplaces, homes, battlefields, colleges, monuments, statues and burial sites. The book contains well over a thousand listings.

My latest project is *In The Footsteps of George Washington*, a chronicle that follows the Father of our Country geographically and chronologically and includes all of the existing places where George slept, fought, lived, ate, drank or was memorialized, from Mount Vernon to Valley Forge to Independence Hall, even George Washington's Bathtub in Berkeley Springs, West Virginia where the natives, with perfectly straight faces, tell visitors that a certain indentation in the rocks is absolutely, positively the spot where Washington partook of the therapeutic waters.

I've also been privileged to assist my brother, Bob, with a book he's been writing. Bob was the Olympic 3-meter springboard diving champion in 1956 and has been commissioned by the Swimming Hall of Fame to write *The History of Diving*. Since he realized I was familiar with every dive in town, whether in New York or Los Angeles, what better person to help?

Life has been a fascinating adventure. After over forty years in the advertising and entertainment business, the switch from "Doctor No" to presidential historian has been remarkably easy and certainly gratifying. I'd always had a passing interest in American history (you know, I was interested in passing) but I was not a serious student. Now I find myself writing, traveling and lecturing, even considered a presidential scholar by some. Mainly my family.

In 1999, I was named one of North Carolina's "Ageless Heroes" in a Blue Cross/Blue Shield program that recognizes senior citizens for after-65 accomplishments, mine for continuing education. It was heart warming although I still have a hard time recognizing myself as a senior citizen (unless there's a discount involved.)

As I look back, the years in the world of advertising and broadcast entertainment were interesting, fun and filled with wonderful associations. The present work as a presidential historian, however, may be less frivolous but seems more important, thus more gratifying. I am involved with people (park rangers, docents, curators), professionals who dedicate themselves to the preservation and maintenance of presidential sites and historic homes, thus helping to perpetuate our great American heritage. I am so very proud to know them and to contribute in my small way in fostering the study of our glorious American history.

I've been lucky, as I've enjoyed good health. I grew up in one of the nation's great small towns, Westfield, New Jersey, in an era that promoted honest values. I was the child of rock-solid, devoted, caring parents. I was privileged to serve my country in World War II (Thank you, President Truman, for sparing me a trip to Japan by landing craft!) and I have been blessed with friends of character and wives of beauty, grace and charm. I've had the honor of working with some of the finest people in advertising and broadcasting, including a future President of the United States. I've brought up children who haven't seen the inside of a jail and I have a grandson carrying on my name.

May William Griffith Clotworthy, II have as entertaining and fulfilling a journey as I've enjoyed.

Special Acknowledgment

It seemed easier, so I chose to write this book in the first person, which is patently unfair to Ralph Daniels, Maurie Goodman and Rick Gitter of NBC's Broadcast Standards Department. They were my leaders who shared all the NBC experiences with me. Their counsel was always sound and inspiring. Their continuing friendship means everything to me.

I am especially grateful to Dr. Richard Gilbert, NBC's religious advisor and resident ethicist. If there is any serious material in this book, you may be sure I've "borrowed" it from his writings. Doctor Gilbert is an intelligent, prescient observer of human nature. We've remained close; he even introduced me to my wife, an act for which I am eternally grateful. It is a privilege to be his friend.

About The Author

William Clotworthy recently completed a forty-two year advertising and broadcasting career encompassing the death throes of network radio, the Golden Years of television and today's fragmented market of networks, cable and home video. As an NBC Page, he witnessed programs featuring the legendary Arturo Toscanini conducting the NBC Symphony, the *Fred Allen Show* and *The Voice of Firestone.* He was there for the television debuts of Howdy Doody, Sid Caesar, Milton Berle and Perry Como.

He moved on to an advertising career in New York and Hollywood as a commercial producer and program supervisor on many family shows, including *Your Hit Parade, You Bet Your Life with Groucho Marx,* and others starring Bing Crosby, Jack Webb, Johnny Carson and Danny Kaye. He spent six unforgettable seasons with *General Electric Theatre* and its host, Ronald Reagan. From 1979 through 1990, he was Director of Program Standards ("Censor") for NBC-TV, responsible for *Saturday Night Live* and *Late Night with David Letterman.*

Mr. Clotworthy's long association with major personalities and successful, sometimes controversial, programs provides an interesting and unusual perspective on the television industry.

Mr. Clotworthy, a native of New Jersey, is a graduate of Syracuse University. He currently lives in Asheville, North Carolina.

www.ingramcontent.com/pod-product-compliance
Lightning Source LLC
Chambersburg PA
CBHW030312290526

45785CB00001B/322